GENDER EQUALITY AND THE OLYMPIC PROGRAMME

Michele K. Donnelly

LONDON AND NEW YORK

First published 2023
by Routledge
4 Park Square, Milton Park, Abingdon, Oxon OX14 4RN

and by Routledge
605 Third Avenue, New York, NY 10158

Routledge is an imprint of the Taylor & Francis Group, an informa business

British Library Cataloguing-in-Publication Data
A catalogue record for this book is available from the British Library

Library of Congress Cataloging-in-Publication Data
Names: Donnelly, Michele K., author.
Title: Gender equality and the Olympic programme / Michele K. Donnelly.
Other titles: Gender equality and the Olympic program
Description: Abingdon, Oxon ; New York City : Routledge, 2023. | Series: Women, sport and physical activity | Includes bibliographical references and index. | Summary: "This innovative study examines the Olympic programme from a critical feminist perspective, to shed new light on the issues of gender and inclusion at the Olympic Games and in the Olympic Movement. Incorporating both quantitative and qualitative data, the book identifies and analyzes the changes - and remaining gender differences - made on the Olympic Programmes for London 2012, and each of the subsequent Summer and Winter Olympic Games (Sochi 2014, Rio 2016, and Pyeongchang 2018), as well as the Tokyo 2020 and Beijing 2022 Games. The book draws on the IOC's own publications, information from International and National Sport Federations, and media sources to describe and explain the IOC's slow and uneven progress toward gender equality at the Olympic Games. This is important reading for any student, researcher, practitioner or policy maker with an interest in the Olympic Games, sport studies, gender studies, women's sport or major events"— Provided by publisher.
Identifiers: LCCN 2022036665 | ISBN 9780367433741 (hardback) | ISBN 9781032416809 (paperback) | ISBN 9781003002741 (ebook)
Subjects: LCSH: Olympics—Social aspects—History—21st century. | International Olympic Committee—History—21st century. | Women Olympic athletes—History—21st century. | Sex discrimination in sports—History—21st century. | Sports—Sex differences. | Critical feminism.
Classification: LCC GV721.5 .D67 2023 | DDC 796.4809—dc23/eng/20221006 LC record available at https://lccn.loc.gov/2022036665

ISBN: 978-0-367-43374-1 (hbk)
ISBN: 978-1-032-41680-9 (pbk)
ISBN: 978-1-003-00274-1 (ebk)

DOI: 10.4324/9781003002741

Typeset in Bembo
by codeMantra

GENDER EQUALITY AND THE OLYMPIC PROGRAMME

This innovative study examines the Olympic programme from a critical feminist perspective, to shed new light on the issues of gender and inclusion at the Olympic Games and in the Olympic Movement.

Incorporating both quantitative and qualitative data, the book identifies and analyses the changes – and remaining gender differences – made on the Olympic Programmes for London 2012, and each of the subsequent Summer and Winter Olympic Games (Sochi 2014, Rio 2016, and Pyeongchang 2018), as well as the Tokyo 2020 and Beijing 2022 Games. The book draws on the IOC's own publications, information from International and National Sport Federations, and media sources to describe and explain the IOC's slow and uneven progress towards gender equality at the Olympic Games.

This is important reading for any student, researcher, practitioner, or policymaker with an interest in the Olympic Games, sport studies, gender studies, women's sport, or major events.

Michele K. Donnelly is Assistant Professor in the Department of Sport Management at Brock University, Canada. Her research agenda is composed of three clearly defined, and often interrelated, lines of sociological inquiry: (1) social inequality, particularly focused on gender; (2) alternative and understudied social practices and subcultures in the realm of sport; and (3) qualitative research methods. Michele is a member of the North American Society for the Sociology of Sport (NASSS).

Women, Sport and Physical Activity

Edited by Elizabeth Pike, University of Hertfordshire, UK

The *Women, Sport and Physical Activity* series showcases work by leading international researchers and emerging scholars that offers new perspectives on the involvement of women in sport and physical activity. The series is interdisciplinary in scope, drawing on sociology, cultural studies, history, politics, gender studies, leisure studies, psychology, exercise science and coaching studies, and consists of two main strands: thematic volumes addressing key global issues in the study of women, sport and physical activity; and sport-specific volumes, each of which offers an overview of women's participation and leadership in a particular sport. Available in this series:

Women's Artistic Gymnastics
Socio-cultural Perspectives
Edited by Roslyn Kerr, Natalie Barker-Ruchti, Carly Stewart and Gretchen Kerr

Women in Rugby
Edited by Helene Joncheray

Improving Gender Equity in Sports Coaching
Edited by Leanne Norman

Women in Judo
Edited by Mike Callan

Gender-Based Violence in Children's Sport
Gretchen Kerr

Gender Equality and the Olympic Programme
Michele K. Donnelly

For more information about this series, please visit: https://www.routledge.com/Women-Sport-and-Physical-Activity/book-series/WSPA

This book is dedicated to all of the women athletes, coaches, fans, officials, and supporters – and their allies – who have led the ongoing struggle for gender equality in sport.

CONTENTS

SERIES EDITOR FOREWORD

Elizabeth C.J. Pike

The Olympic Games are arguably the most high-profile sporting event in the world and, as such, have the capacity to mirror, challenge, and reinforce societal issues in equal measure. It is well-documented that the Olympics were traditionally established as a competition exclusively for men and have a long history of male dominance reflecting the broader trends in most sports for men to have more opportunities to compete, be paid, access media coverage, and progress in coaching, officiating, and management roles.

The gender differences in the Olympics have attracted considerable attention, with surveys demonstrating that there has been very slow progress towards equal numbers of participants and medal-opportunities, while it remains the case that women are significantly under-represented as coaches, officials, and in governance structures. This is perhaps unsurprising given that modern sport has developed from the well-established values of Global North-centric masculinities.

The progress that has been made for women is the outcome of a deliberate focus on gender equality with the IOC responding to calls in the wider women and sport movement to support the ongoing development of a fairer and more equitable system of sport. The IOC subsequently amended its own charter, established a Women and Sport Commission, set gender equality targets, and more recently following its own gender equality review, published gender equality objectives. These are being implemented through concrete actions, such as the Olympic Solidarity support for a Women in Sport High Performance (WISH) pathway delivered by the University of Hertfordshire, UK, to develop and support a sustainable pipeline of women coaches.

While much of this appears positive, there remain questions about the focus on numbers rather than the culture of sport, and on equality rather than equity.

In recent years, the Olympics, as with other high performance sport events, have also reviewed their policies regarding the inclusion or otherwise of transgender, inter-sex, and athletes with differences of sex development.

This book takes as its focus the gendered logic of the Olympic Programme, giving consideration to the focus on, and implications of, the numerical claims and recommendations regarding men and women at the Olympics. Following this, the book considers the conditions of participation for men and women at the Games, and the characteristics and experiences of mixed-gender events.

This is a timely analysis of a rapidly changing landscape. In the short space of time since the manuscript was accepted for publication, there have continued to be gendered differences in the ways that men and women compete in the same sports and events, with new requirements regarding clothing (for example, in skating), and ongoing tensions regarding the inclusion of new women's events (such as the IOC's rejection of a proposal for a new Nordic Combined event for Milan-Cortina 2026). These are illustrative of ongoing, cumulative, points of difference which are being addressed slowly, with a need to continue to monitor their contribution to real gender equality.

Donnelly is a world-leading scholar in the field of gender and Olympic sport. In this book, she invites the reader to reconsider the information provided regarding gender equality on the Olympic Programme, asks challenging questions of anyone committed to true gender equality, and offers constructive guidance for future thinking and action. This book makes an important contribution to the understanding not only of the Olympic Games, but gender equality in sport more broadly, and I whole-heartedly welcome its inclusion in the Routledge *Women, Sport and Physical Activity* series.

ACKNOWLEDGEMENTS

This book would not have happened without the incredible support from Dad (the inimitable Peter Donnelly). He is my first reader, sounding board, and always ready to remind me that the only way to make writing happen is to put my butt in the desk seat. Mum and Alison are also so supportive, and Mum always knows when I might need to *not* be asked about my writing progress. Thank you for everything. Maude made me smile every day and forced me to get outside. Write club meetings with Liz Clarke were invaluable, even when we spent more time talking than writing. Mike Giardina always helps me to believe I might actually be able to do this academic thing. Marla Klinck offered (many, many) suggestions and support throughout the writing process. Last, but definitely not least, Elizabeth Pike and Rebecca Connor were the most patient and encouraging editors I could hope to work with.

ABBREVIATIONS

AIBA	Association Internationale de Boxe Amateur (now International Boxing Association)
ANOC	Association of National Olympic Committees
ASOIF	Association of Summer Olympic International Federations
EOC	European Olympic Committee
FIBA	Fédération Internationale de Basketball
FIFA	Fédération Internationale de Football
FIG	Fédération Internationale de Gymnastique
FIL	Fédération Internationale de Luge
FINA	Fédération Internationale de Natation
FIS	Fédération Internationale de Ski
FIVB	Fédération Internationale de Volleyball
GERP	Gender Equality Review Project
IBSF	International Bobsleigh and Skeleton Federation
ICF	International Canoe Federation
IBA	International Boxing Association
IBU	International Biathlon Union
IF	International Sport Federation
IIHF	International Ice Hockey Federation
IJF	International Judo Federation
INSEE	Institut National de la Statistique et des Études Économiques
IOC	International Olympic Committee
IPC	International Paralympic Committee
ISSF	International Shooting Sport Federation
ISU	International Skating Union
ITF	International Tennis Federation
ITTF	International Table Tennis Federation

ITU	International Triathlon Union
IWF	International Weightlifting Federation
IWRF	International Wheelchair Rugby Federation
NOC	National Olympic Committee
NPC	National Paralympic Committee
OCOG	Organizing Committee of the Olympic Games
UCI	Union Cycliste Internationale
UWW	United World Wrestling
WBSC	World Baseball Softball Confederation
WCF	World Curling Federation
WPIHF	World Para Ice Hockey Federation

1
INTRODUCTION

Introduction: Monobob at Beijing 2022

For the first time in Winter Olympic history, women bobsled athletes at Beijing 2022 were able to compete in two Bobsleigh events: the two-woman event that has been on the Olympic programme since 2002, and a new "monobob" event. Men bobsled athletes have had two events at the Games since the Lake Placid 1932 Games: the two-man event introduced in 1932, and the four-man event that was on the original Olympic Winter sport programme at Chamonix 1924. Women bobsledders have advocated for the inclusion of a four-man event for women for many years. In 2014, the International Bobsleigh and Skeleton Federation (IBSF) allowed women to compete in four-man events on the World Cup circuit, and some women pilots (the athlete who drives the sled), such as Kaillie Humphries, formerly of Canada, now competing for the United States, and American Elana Meyers Taylor, piloted mixed gender sleds. Ivo Ferriani, IBSF president at the time, indicated that there were no limits on the number of women athletes in a sled in the men's four-man event but anticipated that the rule change would affect only the pilot position and not the push positions: "At the moment, we don't have any limits. I think, personally, a woman pilot with three men can be strong" (AP, 2014). Based on the International Olympic Committee's (IOC) promotion of mixed gender events on the Olympic programme, many anticipated that the IBSF's decision would result in the four-man event being a mixed gender event at PyeongChang 2018; however, this was not the case. For Beijing 2022, the IBSF proposed the inclusion of a women's four-man event to the IOC. The IOC rejected the four-man event in favour of a monobob event for women; an event in which one bobsled athlete pushes and drives the sled. Meyers Taylor responded to this decision on Facebook:

DOI: 10.4324/9781003002741-1

> To be fair, this is historic in that it adds another discipline for women's bobsled and that should be celebrated. Personally it's a discipline that weighs heavily in my favor as I am one of the fastest pushing pilots in the world. However, I would be remiss if I did not express my disappointment as myself and many others have been laying the groundwork for 4woman. We will keep fighting.
>
> *(in AP, 2018)*

Canadian pilot, Cynthia Appiah, was even more direct in her critique of the monobob decision:

> Women were shortchanged. We've been advocating for a second event to include more women in the sport for the longest time. This wasn't a fight to just get a second event so that we could win another medal. The point was to progress the sport.
>
> *(in Gillespie, 2021)*

The IOC celebrated that with the addition of women's monobob and a few other events, "Beijing has the highest number of women's events ever [at the Winter Olympic Games]" (IOC, 2022).

The difference in the events available to men (two-man and four-man) and women (two-woman and monobob) bobsledders is not the only difference in the ways that they competed at the Olympic Games. The IBSF allowed 30 teams in the two-man event (60 athletes) and 20 teams in the two-woman event (40 athletes), and 28 teams in the four-man event (112 athletes) and 20 sleds in the women's monobob event (20 athletes). There is some crossover between the events, i.e., men bobsledders who compete in both the two-man and four-man events. In fact, this was a significant part of the appeal of the monobob event; most of the women bobsledders who competed in the inaugural monobob event also competed in the two-woman event. This means that the IBSF and IOC were able to add a women's event to the sport programme without needing to increase the total number of athletes competing in Bobsleigh. Further, there are significant differences in the weight limits for the men's and women's two-man events. The minimum weight of the men's and women's sleds is 170kg, and the maximum weight – including the crew and other racing equipment – is 390kg for men and 330kg for women (before 2015, the maximum weight for the two-woman event was 340kg). Finally, for the women's monobob event, women bobsledders will use a standardized sled:

> Unlike all other sliding events, where teams secure their own sleds and equipment and the teams with the most money to invest tend to do most of the winning, the monobob sleds will be identical to one another — since they'll be paid for by the IBSF. Every sled will be set up the same way, which should mean that the person who best combines a fast start with a clean drive down the ice will more than likely wind up winning.
>
> *(AP, 2018)*

It is noble to introduce a Bobsleigh event that attempts to address some of the inequality in the existing events, as well as serving as a "developmental option" that encourages more countries to invest in training Bobsleigh athletes. According to Ferriani,

> I am sure it will help to develop a young generation because it makes it easier for them to approach the sport. It is sustainable in cost and **it's safe**. You don't need someone behind you to drive. You do not focus on the (bobsled technology). You focus on the driving and the athletic skill.
>
> *(in Gillespie, 2021, my emphasis)*

Since women bobsledders have competed in two-woman events at the Olympic Games since 2002, and in four-man World Cup events since 2018, the suggestion that monobob might be a "safer" Bobsleigh event for women seems unwarranted. It is unclear – and unequal – to expect one women's event to accomplish all of these goals – equality, universality, safety – for all of Bobsleigh. This is especially true when that event only equalizes the number of events for men and women bobsledders, not the number of athletes or their conditions of participation at the Games.

Adams (2010: 225) uses Bobsleigh as an example of women's exclusion from sports in which they previously participated.

> In [male-controlled sporting bureaucracies'] drive to codify certain competitive physical activities as sports and to impose upon them international standards, sporting officials – in some instances on the advice of medical experts – enacted policies that made gender segregation seem normal and natural in sports.

Bobsleigh is one of the "worst cases" as "the institutionalization of the sports led not just to separating the sexes, but to prohibitions against women competing" (Adams, 2010: 225). The first official Bobsleigh rules written in the 1890s required that teams be composed of both men and women athletes. But after being established in 1923, the Fédération Internationale de Bobsleigh et de Tobogganing (now the IBSF) banned women from international competition. Women's participation in Bobsleigh was severely limited for decades until international competition began again in the 1990s. Adams (2010: 226) warns that we cannot assume that women's sport history is always characterized by exclusion and segregation:

> Had women simply been excluded from bobsledding from the beginning, the story would be far less troubling in terms of the way sport has not just reflected but contributed to the discourses and practices through which gender difference is constituted.

The case of Bobsleigh demonstrates the need to examine the Olympic sport programme – Summer and Winter – to better understand gender equality at the

Olympic Games, and the IOC's commitment to gender equality in the Olympic Movement.

In the next sections, I will explain what the Olympic programme is and how it is determined, as well as why it is important to study the Olympic programme. I also briefly introduce the history of women's place on the Olympic programme. Then, I explore how the IOC uses the term "gender equality" and, in the absence of an IOC-provided definition, infer the IOC's meaning. Finally, I outline the contents of each chapter.

What is the Olympic programme?

According to the IOC, "**the Olympic programme is the fundamental core of the Olympic Games** as decisions regarding the programme have an impact on virtually all other areas of the Olympic Games and Olympic Movement" (Agenda 2020, my emphasis). The Olympic programme refers to all of the sports, disciplines, and events included at each edition of the Olympic Games. The IOC (2021b) determines that

> sport is that which is governed by an International Federation (IF). A discipline is a branch of a sport comprising one or more events. [And] An event is a competition in a sport or discipline that gives to rise to a ranking.

For example, the sport of Cycling has four disciplines included on the Summer Olympic programme: BMX, mountain biking, road cycling, and track cycling. Multiple events are held within each discipline, such as the road race and individual time trial in road cycling. The number of medals awarded at any Olympic Games is determined by the number of events approved for the Olympic programme.

Each International Federation (IF) must propose its own event programme to the IOC for each Olympic Games. Through their proposals, IFs often try to increase their presence at the Olympic Games. Specifically, they propose the inclusion of more events and more athletes in their sport than at previous Games. Beginning in 1977, an IOC-appointed Olympic Programme Commission has reviewed the IF proposals and made a recommendation about the sport programme to the IOC Executive Board. The IOC Executive Board makes the final decision about the sport programme, which includes the total number of athletes and events. Currently, the Programme Commission must manage a number of competing interests to develop their recommendations, including

> Develop a programme that maximises the popularity of the Olympic Games while containing costs and complexity;
> Ensure the Olympic programme remains relevant to young people by ensuring innovation and adapting to modern taste and new trends, while respecting the history and tradition of the sports; [...]

Respect the framework and principles outlined in Olympic Agenda 2020 recommendations 9, 10, and 11.

(IOC, 2021c)

The Programme Commission is required to work "in close cooperation with the respective International Federations" as they pursue their seemingly impossible responsibilities: make the Games as popular as possible *and* cost as little as possible; be young, innovative, and new *and* stay true to each sport's history; and address three *Agenda 2020* recommendations. These recommendations are focused on the Olympic sport programme.

Recommendation 9 is to "Set a framework for the Olympic programme", and the IOC (2014) proposed a framework that requires reductions in the numbers of athletes, officials, and events accredited for both the Summer and Winter Olympic Games (more detail about this recommendation is provided in Chapter 2). Recommendation 10 is to "Move from a sport-based to an event-based programme" (IOC, 2014). To accomplish this, the IOC planned for "Regular reviews of the programme to be based on events rather than sports, with the involvement of the International Federations" and adhering to the restrictions on the number of athletes, officials, and events detailed in Recommendation 9 (IOC, 2014). And, Recommendation 11 is to "Foster gender equality" (IOC, 2014). The strategies detailed to accomplish this recommendation are concentrated on the Olympic programme:

1. The IOC to work with the International Federations to achieve 50 per cent female participation in the Olympic Games and to stimulate women's participation and involvement in sport by creating more participation opportunities at the Olympic Games.
2. The IOC to encourage the inclusion of mixed-gender team events.

These *Agenda 2020* recommendations, like the Olympic Programme Commission's complex and contradictory responsibilities, reveal contradictory goals for the Olympic sport programme: decrease the overall number of athletes and events *and* increase the number of opportunities for women athletes and the number of mixed-gender events. The numerical challenges for IFs posed by these contradictory recommendations are detrimental to the pursuit of gender equality (this is explained in detail in Chapter 2).

Despite the information shared by the IOC about the mission of the Olympic Programme Commission, decision-making about the Olympic programme is notoriously undisclosed. In fact, what evaluation criteria are used, how those criteria are assessed, and their relative importance is not made public. According to Morgan (2020),

> The Olympic programme is a hugely complex jigsaw puzzle made more convoluted and difficult by the lack of clarity – and even secrecy –

> demonstrated throughout the process by the IOC and the Federations, who leave it to the last minute to decide their event slate. There do not seem to be any clearly defined parameters used to determine the events that are accepted for Olympic inclusion, leaving Federations and their athletes in limbo until the programme is set in stone. If there were, governing bodies would know exactly what they need to do to achieve a hallowed place at the Games.

There is one minor exception to this lack of information. As part of Recommendation 9, the IOC determined that the Organizing Committee of the Olympic Games (OCOG) – the host committee – would be allowed "to make a proposal for the inclusion of one or more additional events on the Olympic programme for that edition of the Olympic Games" (IOC, 2014). The list of evaluation criteria for these additional events is public, and they are organized into five categories: (1) Olympic proposal; (2) Value added to the Olympic Movement; (3) Institutional matters; (4) Popularity; and (5) Business model (IOC, 2021c). Of the 35 criteria, two include an explicit assessment of the IF in terms of gender equality: "18. Gender equality in the Executive Board (or highest decision making body) of the International Federation"; and "26. Women and Sport Commission (existence of a Women and Sport Commission and representation in decision making body)" (IOC, 2015). Relevant for this project, there are no criteria focused on gender equality in the sport or event itself, such as the numbers of men and women who play, and their conditions of participation.

Why study the Olympic programme?

There is a lot we do not know about how the Olympic sport programme is determined. Rather than making the sport programme less important or interesting to study, this makes it even more necessary to study. Studying the Olympic programme is crucial, first, because it is the most visible aspect of the Olympic Games. What sports are included, which events within those sports, as well as how athletes play those sports (e.g., rules of play, the structure of competition, the physical spaces, and so on), what athletes wear to play, and the equipment they use are all visible to the viewing public. These observable elements send clear messages about the beliefs and values, including those about gender, of those in charge of the Olympic Games. McLachlan (2016: 470) claims,

> not only do the Olympics have a history of excluding people from taking part based on their sex, but the Olympics and its associated symbols, practices, and texts also reproduce or reinforce the meanings (and accompanying hierarchies) that are assigned to each sex.

Who is – and who is not – included at the Olympic Games is most apparent in the composition of the Olympic programme.

Second, the Olympic programme is highly contested terrain; the IOC, IFs, host city Organizing Committees, National Olympic Committees (NOCs), broadcasters, sponsors, and athletes all have specific, sometimes conflicting, interests in its composition. This includes women athletes who continue to struggle to have their events included at the Olympic Games, such as women ski jumpers (who were permitted to compete beginning at Sochi 2014, but are currently limited to competing only on the "normal" size hill, while men compete on both the normal and large hills), and women canoeists who were excluded from the Olympic Games until Tokyo 2020. In particular, IFs invest significant resources in securing a place on the Olympic programme. Dunne (2021) explains,

> Once the Games are under way, the competition between athletes becomes the focus. It's easy to forget the battle a sport has had to go through to be there in the first place. Campaigns can take years and cost an international federation between $100,000 (€84,000) and $500,000 to mount.

The competition for Olympic programme inclusion is intense; for Tokyo 2020, "26 new sports made their case to the IOC. Of these, eight were shortlisted. Five were chosen" (Dunne, 2021). Once included at the Olympic Games, IFs continue to advocate for more athletes and events in their sports (more medals).

Finally, the majority of the IOC's claims about their gender equality achievements are about the Olympic programme. In particular, the IOC regularly highlights the percentage of women athletes at each edition of the Olympic Games to demonstrate progress towards gender equality. In a "Statement on gender equality in the Olympic Movement", the IOC's first stated accomplishment about the Tokyo 2020 Summer Olympic Games asserted, "With female athlete participation of almost 49 per cent, the Olympic Games Tokyo 2020 will be the first gender-equal Olympic Games" (IOC, 2021d). In Chapter 2, I question the claim that including 48.8% women athletes constitutes gender equality. With respect to the Beijing 2022 Winter Olympic Games, the IOC celebrated that "Beijing 2022 is already the most gender-balanced Olympic Winter Games in history, with women accounting for a record 45 per cent of the athletes" before including details about reaching gender balance in particular sports, and the "Highest number of women's events ever" (IOC, 2022). In order to properly assess the IOC's commitment to gender equality, and its actions in pursuit of gender equality, close examination of the Olympic sport programme is required.

Women and/on the Olympic programme

Women's inclusion at the Modern Olympic Games was hotly contested from the beginning. Pierre de Coubertin, the founder of the Modern Olympic Games, made his opposition to women's involvement exceedingly clear. In 1912, he suggested that the inclusion of women at the Olympic Games would be "impractical, uninteresting, unaesthetic, and incorrect". Since that time, the Olympics have been a site for "creating ideologies of male dominance, where images, beliefs and practices of masculine power and superiority are continually replayed and reproduced [...] alongside those that denigrate femininity, women and their sporting activities" (Wamsley & Pfister, 2005: 111). The IOC – along with the IFs – have controlled women's involvement in both quantitative and qualitative terms. Quantitatively, Carpentier and Lefèvre (2006: 1121) identified that

> Women could participate in the Olympic Games only on condition that they in no way cast a shadow over the men. The Executive Board was, for example, very attentive to the ratio of men to women in each sports discipline. In 1927 and 1933, the international federations of gymnastics and swimming were called to order because their ratios were deemed too favourable to the women.[1]

Qualitatively, and in the face of challenges from rival organizations' events, such as the Women's Olympics, the IOC realized that it should allow women's inclusion at the Games. Leigh and Bonin (1977: 77) claim,

> Having decided that it was inevitable for women to want to participate in the national sports of their respective countries, the IOC suggested that the international federations take control of women's activities. The reasons for taking control were somewhat questionable, however. The International Olympic Committee felt that if sports and games were to be promoted for the betterment and improvement of women from the physical and moral point of view, then the soundest line it could adopt was to propose that the international federations properly organize women's sports and see that they competed only in sports suited to their sex.

Despite the IOC's more recent nearly exclusive focus on gender equality in terms of numbers, the history of women's inclusion at the Olympic Games demonstrates concerns not only about the number of women athletes and women's events but also about the conditions of women's participation relative to men in the same sport.

The emphasis on limiting women's participation to "suitable" sports – presumably, sports aligned with dominant ideas about femininity – continued (and, arguably, continues today). According to Boykoff (2016: para. 11), in 1949, IOC vice president Avery Brundage identified specific sports that he deemed suitable: "I think women's events should be confined to those appropriate for women: swimming, tennis, figure skating and fencing but certainly not shot putting". And,

> The [IOC] General Session minutes from the April 1953 meeting in Mexico City read—under the heading of 'Reducing the number of athletes

> and officials'—that 'women not to be excluded from the Games, but only participation in "suitable" sports'.
>
> *(Boykoff, 2016: para. 11)*

McLachlan (2016: 473) identified that inclusion narratives written by sport historians (and, I argue, also by the IOC) reinforce notions of gender difference: "writing about the inclusion of a female event as a significant historic moment is also a way of emphasizing gender difference and reinforcing constructions of 'manliness' and 'womanliness'". In many cases, gender difference is emphasized because women's events are introduced to the Games in ways that differentiate them from the (often already existing) men's events, both in terms of numbers and in terms of the conditions of participation. Pape (2020: 92) argues that as the IOC "began to redefine the general issue of women's participation in terms of a discourse of rights and equity" during the 1970s, "the right of women athletes to equity of participation was premised on the assumption of biological difference, with women's bodies actively constructed as physically able yet inferior to men's". In some ways, the IOC's focus on numbers without a simultaneous focus on conditions of participation effectively leaves unchallenged assumptions about "natural" gender differences that necessitate different conditions of participation for men and women athletes.

Pape (2020) identifies two main ways in which the IOC Programme Commission simultaneously facilitated women's involvement at the Olympic Games, while maintaining the IOC's "gendered logic". She describes this form of change as "*accommodating* women, which leaves an organization's existing gendered structures, practices, and values intact" (Pape, 2020: 82). In the case of the IOC, and I would argue IFs also, gender equality initiatives to date have largely affirmed, rather than transformed, "binary and hierarchical notions of gender difference" (Pape, 2020: 82). Based on her review of IOC documents from the mid-1960 through the mid-1990s, Pape (2020: 96) found that the existence of the Olympic Programme Commission has been integral to the IOC's *accommodating* women approach:

> With structural alignment between the call for greater women's athletic participation (under conditions of segregation) and a formal commission charged with reviewing the Olympic program, the IOC was able to act to formally accommodate women without threatening the organization's gendered logic.

Beginning in 1977, the Olympic Programme Commission oversaw increases in the number of women athletes and women's events at both the Summer and Winter Olympic Games; however, this was not a quick process. According to the IOC's own numbers, in 1988 (ten years after the Programme Commission was established), women athletes comprised 26.1% of all athletes at the Beijing Summer Games and 21.2% of all athletes at the Calgary Winter Games. Women's events made up 30.4% of the Olympic programme at Beijing and 34.8% of the Olympic programme at Calgary (IOC, 2021e). By the beginning of the 2000s (20 years into the operation of the Programme Commission), women athletes comprised 38.2% of all athletes at the Sydney 2000 Summer Games and 36.9% of all athletes at the Salt Lake 2002 Winter Games (IOC, 2021e). In 2000, women's events made up 40% of the Summer Olympic programme and, in 2002, 42.5% of the Winter Olympic programme (IOC, 2021e). Pape (2020: 95) found that "formal rules and criteria often served as an excruciatingly slow avenue for adding new events and sports for women" and, at the same time, "formalization also aided the expansion of women's athletic participation, since rules served as a clear target for external stakeholders, and particularly the IFs". Below, I address the need for rules (or requirements), rather than recommendations, in the IOC's continued commitment to gender equality at the Olympic Games.

While the IOC and, following the IOC's lead, media outlets have paid much attention to the number of women athletes and women's events at the Olympic Games, this should not be the only focus when assessing the IOC's commitment to gender equality. Further, while the focus of this book is on the content of the Olympic programme, the IOC's commitment to gender equality must also be examined in terms of women's participation not only in sport (as athletes) but also in decision-making positions in sport (as coaches, officials, and serving on NOCs, NFs, IFs, and the IOC).

The IOC's accommodation of women athletes at the Olympic Games has been far more successful than its accommodation of women in leadership and decision-making positions in the Olympic Movement, including as members of the IOC itself. However, gender equality in sport participation has not been achieved – either in terms of the numbers of athletes and events or the conditions of participation. Concerningly, there seems to have been a shift in attention to gender equality away from participation to an almost absolute focus on women in sport leadership. In the *Brighton plus Helsinki 2014 Declaration on Women and Sport*, the statement that girls' and women's participation in sport is less than boys' and men's participation in almost all countries, is followed immediately by this claim,

> Despite growing participation of women in sport and physical activity in recent years and increased opportunities for women to participate in domestic and international arenas, increased representation of women in decision making and leadership roles within sport and physical activity has been slow to follow. Women are significantly under-represented in management, administration, coaching and officiating, particularly at the higher levels.
>
> *(IWG Women & Sport, 2014: 2)*

This claim is obviously accurate, and the problem it raises must be solved, but its juxtaposition against girls' and women's increasing sport participation opportunities is not useful. Both of these areas need to be addressed intentionally and consistently in order to achieve gender equality in sport. In a celebration of International Women's Day in 2016, Andrew Ryan, executive director of the Association of Summer Olympic International Federations (ASOIF) said,

> ASOIF and the IOC believe that it is important to understand that the current issue is not only about women in sport but about women in leadership roles. The key word is leadership and one cannot measure the success of equality by pure participation figures, but by looking at the quality of these leadership positions held by women.
>
> *(IOC, 2016a)*

It is necessary to continue to focus on both women's sport participation *and* women's involvement in sport leadership, and to recognize the ways in which these issues are interdependent. "Without women leaders, decision makers and role models and gender sensitive boards and management with women and men within sport and physical activity, equal opportunities for women and girls will not be achieved" (IWG Women & Sport, 2014: 2). It is also necessary to focus on both the quantity *and* quality of women's participation; both by the numbers and beyond the numbers.

My initial interest in closely examining the Olympic sport programme was a result of the celebratory media coverage of, and IOC claims made about, gender equality at the London 2012 Summer Olympic Games. At the Opening Ceremonies, then IOC president, Jacques Rogge claimed that these Games represented "a major boost for gender equality". Some media outlets referred to London 2012 as "The Women's Olympics" (Brown for CNN, 2012) and lauded the "Year of the Woman at the London Games" (Chappell for NPR, 2012). For the most part, media coverage was focused on the number of women competing in London (the largest number of women athletes ever at the Summer Games), and the numbers of women on national teams (e.g., Canada and the United States both sent teams composed of more women than men athletes because Canadian and American women qualified for more team sports than the men). Many reporters – particularly in Great Britain and the United States – also emphasized and celebrated the number of medals won by women athletes on their national teams (relative to the men athletes). It was not only the numbers of women competing that attracted their attention, it was the success of those women athletes – leading *The Daily Mail*'s Martin Samuel (2012) to claim, "Indeed, women do know their place...on the podium".

In the first gender equality audit of the Olympic Games, Peter Donnelly and I wrote:

> Given the triumphal tones of some of the commentary on the important gender equality landmarks achieved at the London 2012 Olympics, it seems an appropriate time – in the spirit of "what's left to do to achieve gender equality at the Olympics?" – to carry out a gender equality audit of these

> Olympics. Our focus is on the basics of the Olympic sports: what differences remain between the ways that men and women athletes are involved in Olympic competitions?
>
> *(Donnelly & Donnelly, 2013)*

In fact, there is much that needs to be done to achieve gender equality at the Olympic Games; men and women athletes continue to have different opportunities at the Games, both in terms of the number of opportunities and their conditions of participation. Focusing on the Olympic programme highlights these remaining differences for two main reasons. First, the IOC and IFs cannot be allowed to claim to have achieved gender equality when they have not. This would not only leave the struggle for gender equality at the Games – waged by women athletes and their advocates for well over a century – unrealized, but it also allows for regression. That is, when the focus moves to something else, and there is no longer intentional, targeted action to achieve gender equality on the Olympic sport programme, movement towards gender equality is not guaranteed. Second, decisions made about the Olympic programme – what and who is included and excluded from the Olympic Games, and how they are included – are incredibly revealing of the gendered logic of the Olympic Movement. The Olympic programme is not natural, neutral, or "just what it is"; it is the result of decisions made by human beings. Exploring the Olympic programme allows for a better appreciation of the binary, hierarchical, difference-focused understanding of gender by which it is informed. The Olympic programme effectively demonstrates the history and legacy of the exclusions of women from certain sports (e.g., Canoe, Greco Roman Wrestling, Nordic Combined, particular apparatus in Artistic Gymnastics, and so on), as well as the deliberate differentiation of the ways that women play some sports that were (often) originally played only by men. IFs design women's versions of a sport to be different from the men's by changing the rules and/or equipment, venue, scoring, and other aspects of playing a sport. This is only possible because of the sex-segregated organization of sport at the Olympic Games. Pape (2020: 100) identified "the inclusion of women athletes [at the Olympic Games] under conditions of segregation established women's lesser status and ability as an organizational norm". In every case where there are differences between men's and women's sport participation, the design is intended to highlight gender differences, avoid direct comparisons between men's and women's performances, and reinforce men's sport and men athletes as better than women's sport and women athletes.

Gender equality and the Olympic programme: What is gender equality?

Whether it is in Recommendation 11 of *Agenda 2020* – "Foster gender equality" – or in celebrations of gender equality achievements at the Olympic Games, the

IOC does not explicitly define "gender equality" or explain how it uses the term. In the absence of an IOC-provided definition, it is necessary to interpret the IOC's definition based on what they recommend, claim, and promote in the name of "gender equality". It may be useful to begin with the *Olympic Charter*, the guiding document of Olympism and the Olympic Movement. Principle 6 of the Fundamental Principles of Olympism is relevant:

> The enjoyment of the rights and freedoms set forth in this Olympic Charter shall be secured without discrimination of any kind, such as race, colour, sex, sexual orientation, language, political or other opinion, national or social origin, property, birth or other status.
>
> *(IOC, 2021a)*

Beneficiaries of the *Olympic Charter*, then, will not be discriminated against based on sex (and other categories of social difference). Current IOC president, Thomas Bach, has claimed, "As the leader of the Olympic Movement, the IOC has an important responsibility to take action when it comes to gender equality – a basic human right of profound importance and a fundamental principle of the Olympic Charter" (IOC, 2018b). At the European Olympic Committees' General Assembly in October 2019, Bach stated, "Gender equality is not just nice to have. It is an important pillar of good governance" (in Gillen, 2019). However, each of these statements is about what gender equality *is* (i.e., a human right, a fundamental principle, and a pillar of good governance) and not about what gender equality *means*.

The IOC's reluctance to state – or, perhaps, a sense that it does not need to state – its definition of gender equality is not new, nor is the academic critique. In 1990, MacNeill recommended that the IOC state its definition of gender equality, its criteria for measuring equality, and specific gender equality policy. The IOC still has not offered a definition of gender equality, nor a specific gender equality policy that addresses processes and decision-making. The IOC has arguably moved towards a more explicit statement of its criteria for measuring gender equality. Specifically, in Recommendation 11, the IOC identifies a goal of "50 per cent female participation in the Olympic Games", "more participation opportunities [for women] at the Olympic Games", and "more mixed-gender team events" (IOC, 2014). Progress towards these goals is measurable or countable, which is important but also limiting. And, as MacNeill stated, gender equality must be approached strategically – with policy – and not only with aspirations and assumptions that progress will be made. The IOC does not address how to achieve these specific gender equality-related goals.

Based on the language used in *Agenda 2020*, and in the promotion of the IOC's gender equality initiatives and accomplishments, it appears that – for the IOC – gender equality means sameness in terms of numbers of men and women. With respect to the Olympic sport programme, the IOC is focused on numerical equality of participation, having the same number of men and women athletes compete at the Games and in the same number of events. There are many examples of this approach in IOC News stories since the release of *Agenda 2020*:

- "The package [of new sports] promotes **gender equality, with each of the five sports having equal numbers of teams for men and women** [...]" (IOC Executive Board Supports Tokyo 2020 Package of New Sports for IOC Session – 1 June, 2016b)
- "The confirmed event programme means **full gender balance [for] the first time at a Winter Olympic event, with the highest number of women's events and women ever competing** at the Winter YOG. This gender equality reflects [...]" (IOC Executive Board Confirms Gender Equality And More Innovation For Winter Youth Olympic Games Lausanne 2020 – 9 July, 2017)
- "These recommendations are just the beginning of the IOC's work towards promoting **gender equality** in the sports world and beyond. While women's participation in sport is growing, with **the ratio of female athletes competing in the Olympic Winter Games PyeongChang 2018 at 42 per cent being a record for the Winter Games**, and, for the first time ever, **equal numbers of women's and men's events on the last day of the Games**, there is still much to be done to create lasting change in competition" (International Women's Day: IOC Setting the Stage for Lasting Change in Sport – 8 March, 2018b)

This is a limited approach to achieving gender equality because the focus on numbers leaves the differences in conditions – or quality – of participation unaddressed and unresolved.

The focus on numbers means that the IOC is intent on achieving gender parity, and not necessarily gender equality. According to Manlosa and Matias (2018),

> Gender parity is a statistical measure that provides a numerical value of female-to-male or girl-to-boy ratio for indicators such as income or education. [...] Gender parity is a useful tool for assessing gender inequality in specific areas, in setting goals, and in assessing change and progress under specific indicators of gender equality.

They clarify that "gender parity is not the same as gender equality and it is important to keep this difference in mind unless we mistake means for ends" (Manlosa & Matias, 2018). In March 2018, the IOC News made a connection between the PyeongChang 2018 Winter Games and International Women's Day: "As the world celebrates International Women's Day, we celebrate the achievements of the female athletes who took centre stage at PyeongChang 2018, a Games which saw the IOC move closer towards the ultimate goal of gender parity" (IOC, 2018a). Although the IOC uses the term "parity" occasionally (the International Paralympic Committee uses it more often), "gender balance" has become one of the most commonly used terms in any discussion of gender equality, and – as demonstrated – both are often used interchangeably with gender equality. Bach is quoted in the European Olympic Committees' (EOC) *Gender Equality Commission Strategy 2019–2021*: "Olympic Agenda 2020, the strategic roadmap for the Olympic Movement, commits everyone in the Olympic family to gender balance" (Thomas Bach in EOC, n.d.). In the same document, EOC Gender Equality Commission president, Sarah Keane, claimed,

> We are almost at equality in terms of Olympic sports participation. We must strive to make similar progress in terms of coaching, officiating and administration. We need to see and believe that there is an equal place for both men and women in all areas of leadership and decision making within the Olympic movement.
>
> *(in EOC, n.d.)*

In March 2020, after announcing that each NOC would be encouraged to send at least one man and one woman athlete to Tokyo 2020 and select both a man and woman athlete to carry the flag in the Opening Ceremonies, an IOC News article declared, "IOC sends extremely strong message that gender balance is a reality at the Olympic Games" (IOC, 2020). Each of these examples reveals an underlying assumption that gender equality is about numbers only, without taking into consideration differences between men's and women's experiences as athletes (and in other roles) at the Olympic Games.

Gender equality refers to *more than* numbers:

> Achieving gender equality [...] involves a substantive shift not only in the proportion of men and women under specific indicators, but in the deeper dimensions of societal norms and sense of identities – to be valued and respected equally, regardless of gender. If gender equality is to be realized, efforts need to go beyond achieving statistics for gender parity.
>
> *(Manlosa & Matias, 2018)*

In a sport context, the *Brighton plus Helsinki 2014 Declaration on Women and Sport* identifies "Equity and equality in society and sport" as its first principle: "Resources, power and responsibility should be allocated fairly and without discrimination on the basis of sex or gender, but such allocation should redress any inequitable balance in the benefits available to women and men" (IWG Women & Sport, 2014). The IOC rarely, if ever, uses the term "gender equity", and I will not elaborate on the distinction between these terms here, as other scholars have done so very eloquently. Notably, in an IOC group on the social networking site, LinkedIn – "Working towards gender equality in sport" – Elyse McDonald, project coordinator at the IOC, wrote, "Equity vs Equality often generates a debate as to what is the most appropriate term. At the IOC, we follow the UN Women definitions and positions" (September, 2020). "UN Women is the United Nations entity dedicated to gender equality and the empowerment of women" (About UN Women) and has been partnered with the IOC since at least 2012. The two organizations signed a Memorandum of Understanding (MoU) to promote "girls' and women's empowerment"; the "renewed The MoU lays out the vision for the next five years of partnership, which will empower women and girls through sport and increase women's leadership and gender equality in the sport industry" (UN Women, 14 November 2017). According to UN Women's "Gender Equality Glossary",

> Gender parity is another term for equal representation of women and men in a given area, for example, gender parity in organizational leadership or higher education. Working toward gender parity (equal representation) is a key part of achieving gender equality, and one of the twin strategies, alongside gender mainstreaming.

And, gender equality or "equality between women and men"

> refers to the equal rights, responsibilities and opportunities of women and men and girls and boys. Equality does not mean that women and men will become the same but that women's and men's rights, responsibilities and opportunities will not depend on whether they are born male or female. Gender equality implies that the interests, needs and priorities of both women and men are taken into consideration, recognizing the diversity of different groups of women and men. Gender equality is not a women's issue but should concern and fully engage men as well as women. Equality between women and men is seen both as a human rights issue and as a precondition for, and indicator of, sustainable people-centered development.

By UN Women's definitions, gender parity is only one part of achieving gender equality. That is, gender equality is about *more than* numbers and representation.

Connell (2005: 1801) identifies, "Moving toward a gender-equal society involves profound institutional change as well as change in everyday life and personal conduct" (Connell, 2005: 1801). The almost exclusively numerical focus of the IOC's commitment to gender equality effectively reinforces that women are *accommodated* at the Olympic Games and in the Olympic Movement. By emphasizing gender parity, the IOC avoids any transformation to its binary and hierarchical gendered logic. The foundational belief underlying the IOC's approach to gender equality is that there are essential differences between men and women (gender) and males and females (sex) that necessitate sex-segregated competition. Ritchie (2003: 81–82) explains, "Sport as an institutionalized social practice has vigilantly reinforced the idea that men's and women's 'natural' constitutions and, by implication, their social and cultural practices are determined by their bodies' respective biological, physiological or anatomical structures".

Pape (2020: 101–102) concluded that under the conditions of sex segregation, "Women athletes succeeded in formalizing their access [to the Olympic Games], but at the price of reinforcing their distinctiveness and inferiority", and that "women athletes continue to experience entrenched forms of discrimination and devaluation, revealing the challenges that accompany access won under conditions of essential difference". The differences between men's and women's participation at the Olympic Games go far beyond their relative number of athletes and events. Women's *accommodation* – with a focus on numerical representation – has been designed to differentiate men's and women's conditions of participation, by institutionalizing differences in rules, equipment, uniforms, and so on. While it may be possible to achieve gender parity using this approach, it is not possible to achieve gender equality.

Recommendations, not requirements

In addition to the lack of an IOC-provided definition of gender equality, one of the most significant challenges related to the assessment of gender equality and the Olympic programme is that the IOC has not established any policy beyond the values enshrined in the *Olympic Charter* and recommendations made in *Agenda 2020* and elsewhere. The lack of policy means that responsibility for implementing the IOC's recommendations has been downloaded to other organizations within the Olympic Movement. With respect to the Olympic programme, this is primarily the IFs, whose work is made especially difficult when presented with contradictory recommendations by the IOC (such as decrease the total number of athletes and increase the number of women athletes). In some cases, this has led IFs to make decisions that do not promote gender equality, not when gender equality is understood as concerning both men and women. Although Bach has said, "Gender equality is not a women's issue; gender equality is a human right of profound importance to everyone on earth" (in IOC, 2016a), the absence of guidance for IFs about *how* to implement the IOC's recommendations has resulted in a number of IFs taking away opportunities from men athletes to add opportunities for women athletes (e.g., removing men's events to add women's events) in the name of gender equality and compliance with *Agenda 2020*. This aligns with Larsson's (2014: 230) claim that

> interventions and support in the name of 'gender equality' since 1989 [in Sweden] have been made first and foremost 'for girls and women'. In fact, the concept of 'gender' seems chiefly to mean 'girls' or 'women'. For instance, when sports representatives discuss 'gender', it is mainly about the conditions under which *girls and women* participate in sport [...]. Boys' and men's sport is rarely designated as a 'gender' issue. Instead, it serves as the – often implicit – normative foundation for reflection on girls' and women's sport. Thus, not including boys' and men's sport in a discussion on gender equality is effectively a way of not challenging gender power relations.

Treating gender equality as though it is a 'women's issue' at the Olympic Games reinforces the notion of men athletes and events as the 'norm', even when decisions made using this perspective disadvantage men athletes. It is also unclear if there are consequences for IFs (and other organizations) that do not meet the IOC's gender equality recommendations, or if there are rewards for those who do meet them. Without this, IFs are left to decide which of the IOC's recommendations – about gender equality and other issues – they choose to prioritize. On the few occasions when the IOC has established policy related to gender equality, such as determining in 1991 that any new sport on the Olympic programme must include women's events, it has been successful. However, this requirement has not been applied to sports that were already on the Olympic programme before 1991, *and* it does not address the different conditions of men's and women's participation in many sports, which limits the focus to gender parity and not gender equality.

In the following chapters, I use specific examples from both the Summer and Winter Olympic sport programmes – and, in some cases, from the Paralympic Games programme as well – to compare the IOC's claimed commitments to gender equality to the reality at the Olympic Games. In Chapter 2, "The Olympic programme by the numbers: Quantitative gender inequalities", I assess the IOC on its own terms. That is, in terms of gender parity on the Olympic programme. It is necessary to contextualize the numbers both in terms of the IOC's claims about gender equality at the Olympic Games, and in terms of the contradictory numerical recommendations in *Agenda 2020* that require IFs to simultaneously reduce their total number of athletes and increase opportunities for women athletes. Assessment of the numbers includes a few different categories of numbers, including the number of men and women athletes who participate at the Games, each IF's athlete quota numbers for the Games, the number of events that are available to men and women athletes, and the numbers within specific sports. The trend among IFs – with implicit support from the IOC – has been to eliminate places for men athletes and men's events to add places for women athletes and women's events. I argue that this is not a reasonable way to achieve gender equality. In Chapter 3, "The Olympic programme *beyond* the numbers: Qualitative gender inequalities", I focus on the conditions of participation for men and women athletes at the Olympic Games. The Olympic programme is rife with examples of *within* sport typing – a result of decisions made to differentiate the ways that men and women compete in the same sports and events. There are many categories of gendered differences, including differences in the length of races, available weight categories, the height, weight, size, and spacing of equipment and the size of venue, and a final category that includes differences in judging, rules, and uniforms. In each case where sports are gender differentiated, women's sport is designed to be a lesser version of men's sport. In these chapters about both the quantitative and qualitative gender inequalities **on** the Olympic programme, I also include examples of sports and events that are not gender differentiated. Internal contradictions **on** the Olympic programme – where some events are constructed to be different for men and women athletes, while men and women compete in similar events in the same ways – reinforce the need to identify and explain the remaining examples of *within* sport typing.

Chapters 4 and 5, "Encourage the inclusion of mixed-gender team events" address this IOC-proposed strategy to "foster gender equality" at the Olympic Games. In Chapter 4, I focus on "Sport-specific mixed gender and open competition events". These include some of the most established mixed-gender events on the Olympic programme, such as the Figure Skating ice dance and Pairs events, and Equestrian events. In Chapter 5, the focus is "Mixed gender relay and team events", which includes many of the mixed-gender events that have been added since the release of *Agenda 2020*. In both chapters, I identify the common characteristics of mixed-gender events, such as the fact that they are often an additional event in a sport that does not require additional athletes, and that many mixed-gender events reinforce, rather than challenge or transform, existing gender inequalities in a sport. Ultimately, the current organization of mixed-gender events on the Olympic programme does not "foster gender equality". In the final chapter, I draw connections between the various categories of gender inequality detailed in the discussion of quantitative and qualitative differences, and mixed gender events.

Note

1 Carpentier and Lefèvre (2006: Endnote 42) detail the "too favourable to women" numbers: "The International Gymnastics Federation authorized the participation of 16 to 18 women and seven or eight men at the 1928 Olympic Games. The swimming programme of the 1936 Olympic Games comprised nine events for men and seven for women".

References

About UN Women (n.d.). https://www.unwomen.org/en/about-us/about-un-women. Retrieved: 15 October, 2019.

Adams, Mary Louise (2010). From mixed-sex sport to sport for girls: The feminization of figure skating. *Sport in History*, 30(2), 218–241.

Associated Press (25 September 2014). FIBT rules women can compete in 4-man bobsled. https://www.cbc.ca/sports/fibt-rules-women-can-compete-in-4-man-bobsled-1.2777678. Retrieved: 28 May, 2022.

Associated Press (19 July 2018). Women getting a second bobsled event at 2022 Olympics. https://www.usatoday.com/story/sports/olympics/2018/07/19/women-getting-a-second-bobsled-event-at-2022-olympics/36984407/. Retrieved: 28 May, 2022.

Boykoff, Jules (July 26, 2016). The forgotten history of female athletes who organized their own Olympics. https://www.bitchmedia.org/article/forgotten- history-female-athletes-who-organized-their-own-olympics. Retrieved: 8 February, 2019.

Brown, Sarah (10 August 2012). London 2012: The women's Olympics? *CNN*. https://www.cnn.com/2012/08/10/sport/london-olympics-women/index.html. Retrieved: 1 September, 2012.

Carpentier, Florence & Jean-Pierre Lefèvre (2006). The modern Olympic Movement, women's sport and the social order during the inter-war period. *The International Journal of the History of Sport*, 23(7), 1112–11127.

Chappell, Bill (10 August 2012). Year of the woman at the London games? For Americans, It's true. https://www.npr.org/sections/thetorch/2012/08/10/158570021/year-of-the-woman-at-the-london-games-for-americans-its-true. Retrieved: 1 September, 2012.

Connell, R. W. (2005). Change among the gatekeepers: Men, masculinities, and gender equality in the global arena. *Signs: Journal of Women in Culture and Society*, 30(3), 1801–1821.

Donnelly, Peter & Michele K. Donnelly (2013). *The London 2012 Olympics: A Gender Equality Audit*. Centre for Policy Studies Research Report. Toronto: Centre for Sport Policy Studies, Faculty of Kinesiology and Physical Education, University of Toronto.

Dunne, Frank, (1 July 2021). Inclusion in the Olympic Games remains the Holy Grail for even the most established sports. https://www.sportbusiness.com/2021/07/inclusion-in-the-olympic-games-remains-the-holy-grail-for-even-the-most-established-sports/. Retrieved: 2 July, 2021.

European Olympic Committees (n.d.). *EOC Gender Equality Commission Strategy 2019–2021*. https://www.olympiakomitea.fi/uploads/2019/11/c3acf2a2-eoc-gender-equality-strategy.pdf.

Gillen, Nancy (25 October 2019). EOC General Assembly focuses on gender equality as new constitution approved. https://www.insidethegames.biz/articles/1086339/eoc-general-assembly-gender-equality. Retrieved: 3 November, 2019.

Gillespie, Kerry (4 December, 2021). 'Women were shortchanged.' Why bobsledding's idea of equality doesn't add up. https://www.thestar.com/sports/olympics/analysis/2021/12/04/women-w...-shortchanged-why-bobsleddings-idea-of-equality-doesnt-add-up.html. Retrieved: 28 May, 2022.

IOC (2014). *Olympic Agenda 2020: 20 +20 Recommendations*. Lausanne: International Olympic Committee.

IOC (June 2015). Olympic programme – Host city proposal: Evaluation criteria for events. https://stillmed.olympics.com/media/Document%20Library/OlympicOrg/IOC/Who-We-Are/Commissions/Olympic-Programme/Olympic-programme-Host-city-proposal-Evaluation-criteria.pdf

IOC (2016a). IOC steps it up for gender equality on International Women's Day. https://www.olympic.org/news/ioc-steps-it-up-for-gender-equality-on-international-women-s-day. Retrieved: 15 October, 2019.

IOC (1 June 2016b). IOC executive board supports Tokyo 2020 package of new sports for IOC session. https://olympics.com/ioc/news/ioc-executive-board-supports-tokyo-2020-package-of-new-sports-for-ioc-session. Retrieved: 15 June, 2016.

IOC (9 July 2017). IOC Executive Board confirms gender equality and more innovation for Winter Youth Olympic Games Lausanne 2020. https://olympics.com/ioc/news/-ioc-executive-board-confirms-gender-equality-and-more-innovation-for-winter-youth-olympic-games-lausanne-2020. Retrieved: 3 February, 2018.

IOC (8 March 2018a). Women and gender parity in the spotlight at Pyeongchang 2018. https://www.olympic.org/news/women-and-gender-parity-in-the-spotlight-at-pyeongchang-2018. Retrieved: 19 January, 2021.

IOC (8 March 2018b). International Women's Day: IOC setting the stage for lasting change in sport. https://olympics.com/ioc/news/international-women-s-day-ioc-setting-the-stage-for-lasting-change-in-sport. Retrieved: 19 January, 2021.

IOC (4 March 2020). IOC sends extremely strong message that gender balance is a reality at the Olympic Games. https://olympics.com/ioc/news/ioc-sends-extremely-strong-message-that-gender-balance-is-a-reality-at-the-olympic-games. Retrieved: 10 March, 2020.

IOC (2021a). *Olympic Charter* – In force as from 8 August 2021. https://stillmed.olympics.com/media/Document%20Library/OlympicOrg/General/EN-Olympic-Charter.pdf?_ga=2.69970328.928947499.1654486323-2109730613.1619993075.
IOC (2021b). Sports, programme and results. https://olympics.com/ioc/faq/sports-programme-and-results.
IOC (2021c). Olympic programme commission. https://olympics.com/ioc/olympic-programme-commission.
IOC (9 February 2021d). IOC Statement on gender equality in the Olympic Movement. https://olympics.com/ioc/news/ioc-statement-on-gender-equality-in-the-olympic-movement. Retrieved: 12 February, 2021.
IOC (December 2021e). Factsheet – Women in the Olympic Movement. https://stillmed.olympics.com/media/Documents/Olympic-Movement/Factsheets/Women-in-the-Olympic-Movement.pdf
IOC (14 February 2022). Beijing 2022 sets new records for gender equality. https://olympics.com/ioc/news/beijing-2022-sets-new-records-for-gender-equality. Retrieved: 1 March, 2022.
IWG Women & Sport (2014). *Brighton plus Helsinki 2014 Declaration on Women and Sport.* Adopted during the 6th IWG World Conference on Women and Sport in Helsinki, Finland from June 12–15, 2014.
Larsson, Hakan (2014). Can gender equality become an encumbrance: The case of sport in the Nordic countries. In Jennifer Hargreaves & Eric Anderson (Eds.), *Routledge Handbook of Sport, Gender and Sexuality* (pp. 226–234). London, New York: Routledge.
Leigh, Mary H. & Thérèse M. Bonin (1977). The pioneering role of Madam Alice Milliat and FSFI in establishing international track and field competition for women. *Journal of Sport History*, 4(1), 72–83.
Manlosa, Aisa & Denise Margaret Matias (2018). International Women's Day 2018 – From gender parity to gender equality: Changing women's lived realities. *The Current Column*, 5 March 2018. German Development Institute.
McLachlan, Fiona (2016). Gender politics, the Olympic Games, and Road Cycling: The case for critical history. *The International Journal of the History of Sport*, 33(4), 469–483.
Morgan, Liam (3 December 2020). Liam Morgan: IOC decision on Paris 2024 programme will bring to an end a convoluted and confusing process. https://www.insidethegames.biz/articles/1101503/paris-2024-new-events-ioc-olympics. Retrieved: 23 January, 2021.
Pape, Madeleine (2020). Gender segregation and trajectories of organizational change: The underrepresentation of women in sport leadership. *Gender & Society*, 34(1), 81–105.
Ritchie, Ian (2003). Sex tested, gender verified: Controlling female sexuality in the age of containment. *Sport History Review*, 34, 80–98.
Samuel, Martin (10 August 2012). Indeed, women do know their place…on the podium. *Mail Online*. https://www.dailymail.co.uk/sport/olympics/article-2186693/London-2012-Olympics-Womens-place-podium--Martin-Samuel.html. Retrieved: 1 September, 2012.
UN Women (n.d.). Gender equality glossary. https://trainingcentre.unwomen.org/mod/glossary/view.php?id=36.
UN Women (14 November 2017). UN Women and the International Olympic Committee renew partnership on sport for gender equality. unwomen.org. Retrieved: 29 October, 2019.
Wamsley, Kevin & Gertrude Pfister (2005). Olympic men and women: The politics of gender in the modern games. In Kevin Young and Kevin B. Wamsley (Eds.), *Global Olympics: Historical and Sociological Studies of the Modern Games* (pp. 103–125). London: Elsevier.

2

A QUANTITATIVE ANALYSIS OF GENDER INEQUALITIES AND THE OLYMPIC PROGRAMME

By the numbers

Introduction

Numbers are central to the International Olympic Committee's (IOC) approach to gender equality on the Olympic programme. Specifically, the IOC measures and promotes its gender equality achievements almost exclusively in terms of the number or percentage of women and women's events at the Olympic Games. I have been closely following the IOC's claims about achievements related to gender equality since the London 2012 Summer Games. At London 2012, the IOC celebrated three significant accomplishments related to gender equality: (1) A higher percentage of women athletes than at any previous Summer Olympic Games (4,835 women athletes comprised 44.3% of all athletes); (2) with the inclusion of women's events in Boxing, women athletes competed in every sport at the Games; and (3) the IOC claimed that every country competing at London 2012 included women athletes on their teams.

Each of these claims – including then president of the IOC, Jacques Rogge's (2012) statement that the London 2012 Games represented "a major boost for gender equality" – warrant scrutiny. In part, investigating these claims is necessary in order to better understand what the IOC means when it talks about gender equality. And, it is crucial to judge the veracity of the IOC's claims about gender equality; both in terms of truthfulness and completeness. Using the London 2012 claims as an example, it is accurate that the highest number and proportion of women athletes relative to men athletes competed at these Games. It must be noted, though, that 116 years after the first modern Olympic Games, and 112 years of women's inclusion at the Summer Olympic Games, the IOC was celebrating the fact that 44.3% of all athletes at London 2012 were women. In terms of gender equality – if this is understood as equal numbers of men and women – the Olympic Games still had a lot of work to accomplish.

DOI: 10.4324/9781003002741-2

At London 2012, women did, for the first time, compete in all sports on the Olympic programme. However, women athletes were only able to compete in three weight categories in Boxing, while there were ten weight categories for men athletes. The total numbers of men and women athletes were also significantly different; a difference that is not entirely accounted for by the different number of weight categories. Specifically, there were 250 men athletes and 36 women athletes in Boxing. Although women were no longer excluded from competing in Boxing at the Games, it is challenging to frame their participation in terms of gender equality, especially equality defined in exclusively quantitative terms. Further, while women competed in both Canoe/Kayak and Wrestling at London 2012 (and previous Summer Olympic Games), they were excluded from one of the disciplines of each of these sports; women paddlers competed only in Kayak (and not Canoe) events, and women wrestlers competed only in freestyle (and not Greco Roman) events. Women's inclusion, then, requires attention to the specific ways in which women are included (and excluded) in sports on the Olympic programme.

Similarly, the claim that each National Olympic Committee (NOC) sent women to London 2012 is only partially accurate. In fact, no countries excluded women from their London-bound teams. Rogge successfully pressured three countries – Brunei, Qatar, and Saudi Arabia – to include women athletes in their national teams for the first time. In fact, two countries sent teams composed only of men athletes: Barbados sent six athletes and Nauru sent two athletes to London. These very small national teams only had men athletes qualify to compete at the Games. Bhutan sent a team of only two women athletes to London. Notably, no teams were – or are – required to send both men and women athletes to the Olympic Games. Despite its stated commitments to gender equality, the IOC has not instituted any gender-based requirements for NOCs.

Taken together, a closer analysis of the IOC's claims about gender equality achievements at London 2012 raises the need to closely scrutinize how the IOC speaks about gender equality. That is, numbers alone cannot offer a complete picture of gender equality, and gender inequality, at the Olympic Games. In this chapter, I provide necessary context for the numbers (of athletes, events, and sports) at the Olympic Games, and address the importance of evaluating the IOC on its own terms by introducing the concept of gender parity (as one part of gender equality). I then explain what is known about the numbers at the most recent Summer and Winter Olympic Games and Paralympic Games, and demonstrate that this exclusive focus on numbers is an unnecessarily limited way to understand and pursue gender equality at the Olympic Games. Finally, I explore the very concerning trend of IFs eliminating places for men athletes and men's events in order to add places for women athletes and women's events in the name of "gender equality".

A focus on numbers

The primary purpose of this book is to demonstrate that assessing gender equality on the Olympic programme must recognize that gender equality is about *more than* gender parity. Specifically, UNESCO's definitions reveal that gender parity may contribute to achieving gender equality; however, it is not synonymous with gender equality.

> Gender equality: it's about equal status! Women and men can fully realize their fundamental rights and have equal opportunities and rights to access and contribute to national, political, economic, social and cultural development, and to benefit from the results.
>
> *(Gender Wire, UNESCO, 2015)*

Gender parity is about equality in exclusively numerical terms, without taking into account access to, and the conditions of, participation.

> Gender parity: it's about numbers! The goal is to reach a balanced ration of women and men (ideally, 50/50) in terms of representation and participation at all levels. It's a quantitative objective and not a qualitative one. This is why it represents only a limited way to measure gender equality.
>
> *(Gender Wire, UNESCO, 2015)*

To focus on numbers – gender parity – is to evaluate the IOC on its own terms. That is, the IOC has consistently set numbers-based goals related to gender equality; most often in terms of women's representation in decision-making positions.

At the 1994 Centennial Olympic Congress in Paris, the IOC started to seriously consider gender inequality at the Olympic Games, and in the Olympic Movement more broadly. Specifically, the IOC set recommendations to address the low numbers of women in governing and administrative bodies of the Olympic Movement, including the IOC itself.

> The NOCs, IFs [International Sport Federations], National Federations and sporting bodies belonging to the Olympic Movement must set the objective of reserving at least 20% of decision-making positions for women (particularly in all executive and legislative bodies) within their structures by the end of 2005.
>
> *(IOC, 2016a)*

These sporting bodies are responsible for determining the Olympic programme (IFs) and determining which athletes are sent to the Olympic Games (NOCs). According to the IOC, by 2005, 46% of NOCs who participated in an IOC survey had less than 20% women on their Executive Boards, and 7.4% of NOCs had no women on their Executive Board. There has been some improvement with respect to the number of women in decision-making positions; however, overall, women continue to be seriously underrepresented in sport organizations – inside and outside the Olympic Movement – globally. Despite this lack of success, the IOC claimed, "A number of NOCs and IFs have already shown their willingness to work on achieving parity between men and women" (2016a). This is an example of the IOC using parity and equality interchangeably when referring to gender. It also highlights two consistent elements of the IOC's approach to gender equality: (1) Recommendations (or targets); and (2) focused on numbers.

Adriaanse (2017) emphasizes the need to distinguish between quotas – which are mandated, definite, and result in sanctions for non-compliance – and targets. Targets "are more voluntary in nature, reflecting aspirational goals that the organisation hopes to achieve. They cannot be legally enforced and usually do not carry sanctions if not achieved" (Adriaanse, 2017). The IOC has not implemented quotas – only targets, often framed as recommendations, as in *Agenda 2020* – related to gender equality. (The one exception, beginning in 1991, required all new sports added to the Olympic programme to include both men's and women's events).

Targets have operated much more successfully in terms of the Olympic programme. That is, women athletes and women's events were added more quickly than women in decision-making positions. By Atlanta 1996, over 3,500 women athletes competed in 97 events (comprising 34% of all athletes and almost 36% of all events) (IOC, 2021b). These increases were so significant – and relatively quick – that the 1996 Atlanta Summer Olympic Games were the first to be referred to as the "Women's Games"/"Games of the Woman", or, in the context of the United States, the "Gender Equity Games" (Tuggle & Owen, 1999). This celebration of the Games relied exclusively on their featuring more women athletes and women's events than any previous Games; women continued to be excluded from a number of sports and events, and for those they did compete in, often competed using different rules, equipment, uniforms, and so on; and, most relevant to this discussion, in smaller numbers than men athletes in equivalent events. In 2014, when preparing *Agenda 2020*, Recommendation 11 ("achieve 50 per cent female participation in the Olympic Games" (IOC, 2014a)) made it clear that the IOC had not yet achieved gender equality – or gender parity – at the Olympic Games.

Semi-regular updates to the IOC's "Women and the Olympics" Factsheet include the percentage of women athletes and women's events at each Summer and Winter Olympic Games. These reveal increasing numbers of women athletes and women's events beginning with the 1904 St. Louis Summer Games and the 1928 St. Moritz Winter Games, with some exceptions, and consistent increases since the 1960 Rome Summer Games and the 1972 Sapporo Winter Games (IOC, 2021b). During that same time, the numbers of men athletes and men's events at the Games have also increased. According to the IOC, the pursuit of having 50% women athletes and 50% women's events at the Games may work to achieve both parity and equality:

> The IOC is not only seeking to achieve statistical parity, but also understands that every opportunity provided for women's sport and female

> athletes in the Olympic Games has a flow-on impact for the promotion of gender equality, and the opportunities that are given to women' athletes around the world.
>
> (*IOC, 2020a,* Promotion of women in sport through time)

The IOC seems to suggest that the addition of women's events to the Olympic programme will have a trickle-down effect on women's sports; that is, it will lead to increased investment in, and opportunities for, women in (Olympic) sports. This allows the IOC to maintain that it is committed to gender equality, without encroaching on the autonomy of IFs with respect to making decisions about the organization and rules of their sports.

However, returning to the discussion of parity and equality. The IOC's promotion of gender equality in terms of "statistical parity" – often referred to as gender balance – seems to be its almost exclusive focus. In its reporting about gender equality at the Tokyo 2020 and Beijing 2022 Games, the IOC refers consistently to achievements in terms of "gender balance". For example, the IOC (2021b, my emphasis) claims, "Tokyo 2020 had the most **gender-balanced** athlete participation to date, with female athletes accounting for 48 per cent of the total", and identifies three additional gender equality achievements:

- Four IFs moved to gender-balanced events for the first time (Canoe, Rowing, Shooting and Weightlifting).
- Three disciplines achieved gender balance (BMX racing, mountain biking and freestyle wrestling).
- Six IFs moved to gender-balanced athlete quotas (Canoe, Judo, Rowing, Sailing, Shooting and Weightlifting).

Prior to Tokyo 2020, the IOC demonstrated that it uses "gender equality" and "gender parity" interchangeably. With respect to the 2018 Youth Olympic Games in Buenos Aires, the IOC announced that it had made Olympic history when the Executive Board approved the athlete quotas, "which, for the first time in Olympic history, achieve gender equality on the sports programme with 1,893 women and 1,893 men set to compete" (IOC, 2015). In fact, although the IOC continues to use the term "gender equality" to describe its overall commitment, it consistently uses "gender balance" when describing the actual achievements made at the Games (and in leadership). Arguably, this is more accurate because so many of those achievements are exclusively about numbers, and making the number of men and women athletes, and men's and women's events, more similar – more "balanced".

The International Paralympic Committee (IPC) has adopted similar language to the IOC with respect to its gender equality achievements. President Andrew Parsons has explicitly used the term "gender parity" when referring to the number of athletes competing at the Games. The number of women athletes increased nearly 11% between the Rio 2016 and Tokyo 2020 Summer Paralympic

Games to a record 1,853 women athletes; 42% of all athletes competing at Tokyo 2020. According to Parsons (IPC, 2021a):

> It is absolutely fantastic news that more women than ever before will compete at the Tokyo 2020 Paralympic Games and a lot of credit needs to go to NPCs and International Federations for ensuring this continued growth in numbers. Although we are still someway short of gender parity, we are heading in the right direction with the number of women competing at the Paralympics almost doubling since the Sydney 2000 Paralympics.

Similarly, Parsons (IPC, 2022) celebrated that the Beijing 2022 Paralympic Winter Games would include more women athletes than any previous Winter Paralympic Games:

> I am delighted to see that the number of female Para athletes has grown tremendously, reaching record levels. Much work still needs to be done to achieve gender parity but having increased female participation significantly at the Winter Games in the last 20 years, shows we are heading in the right direction.

In Beijing, the 138 women athletes comprised almost 24.5% of all athletes. Both the Summer and Winter Paralympic Games have shorter histories than the Olympic Games; the first games for people with disabilities were held at Stoke Mandeville Hospital in the United Kingdom in 1948, and Rome 1960 was the first time the Summer Games were held in the same venues as the Olympic Games (Summer Paralympic Games Overview, n.d.). The Winter Games were first held in 1976, and in the same venues as the Olympic Games for the first time at Albertville 1992 (Winter Paralympic Games Overview, n.d.).

Women have been included in the Paralympic Games since their inception; however, women continue to be significantly underrepresented as both athletes and decision makers (Dean et al., 2021). At the Paralympic Games, the sport programme includes fewer opportunities for women athletes in terms of the number of sports they are able to participate in (e.g., Football 5-a-side is a team sport for men only), the number of events, and the number of ability-based classification categories within each event (Houghton et al., 2018). In their study of women in the Paralympic Movement, Dean et al. (2021: 3) addressed their research team's struggle to assess women's involvement in terms of more than numbers:

> When first undertaking this work, it was our hope, as well, to be able to interrogate more broadly how gender is constructed, understood, and enacted within the Paralympic Movement. We had many discussions as a team about the value of "counting the women." However, as the research progressed, it became clear to us that although the IPC and other stakeholders made aspirational statements about commitments to diversity,

> inclusion, and social justice in high-level strategy documents, the documents that spoke of specific initiatives and strategies referenced much more limited concepts, such as gender balance and gender parity, and reported on items such as increasing the medals available to women at the Games.

Dean et al. (2021: 7) identify two main concerns with this approach: (1) It limits the discussion of gender equity and equality to the binary categories of men and women; and (2) their findings demonstrated that "The rhetoric of gender balance is there, but the practice is not".

Parity should be understood as part of the discussion about gender equality, but should not be where the discussion ends. According to the Institut National de la Statistique et des Études Économiques (INSEE) (n.d.),

> Parity means that each gender is represented equally. It is an instrument at the service of equality, which consists in ensuring the access of women and men to the same opportunities, rights, opportunities to choose, material conditions while respecting their specificities. The notion of parity constitutes the foundation of policies to combat the disparities between women and men.

It is necessary to move beyond numbers as a means to assess gender equality; however, in this chapter, I adopt this numerical approach to explore how the IOC most commonly addresses gender equality. This is the case in terms of its recommendations related to gender equality, and the promotion of its actions taken towards achieving gender equality. In the following section, I explain an important aspect of the numerical context of the Olympic Games. That is, the constraints placed on decision-making related to the Olympic programme, and particularly the addition of events and sports to the Olympic programme.

Agenda 2020 – numerical recommendations in conflict

The IOC's commitment to gender equality in numerical terms is particularly apparent in Recommendation 11 of *Agenda 2020*: "Foster gender equality". The first strategy proposed to achieve this recommendation is:

> The IOC to work with the International Federations to achieve 50 per cent female participation in the Olympic Games and to stimulate women's participation and involvement in sport by creating more participation opportunities at the Olympic Games.
>
> *(IOC, 2014a)*

This recommendation refers solely to the number of participation opportunities; that women should make up 50% of the athletes at the Games, and that there need to be more opportunities for women to participate in and be involved at the Games (possibly as coaches, officials, and in other non-athlete roles). The focus, then, is on one clearly defined numerical goal (50%) about the proportion of women athletes participating at the Games, and one less clearly defined, but still uniquely numerical, goal. Not addressed are other crucial elements of gender equality, including those focused on the conditions of men's and women's participation at the Olympic Games, as well as the relative status of women occupying non-athlete roles. Qualitative differences between men's and women's participation are the focus of the next chapter.

"Foster gender equality" is one of two significant recommendations that refer to numbers (of people and events) at the Olympic Games. Specifically, Recommendation 9, "Set a framework for the Olympic programme" addresses the total number of athletes, officials, and events that should be allowed at each edition of the Summer and Winter Olympic Games. For the Summer Games, the IOC recommends limiting the numbers to 10,500 athletes, 5,000 accredited coaches and athletes' support personnel, and 310 events (2014a). This requires a considerable decrease in the number of athletes from the previous two Summer Games: 11,237 athletes at Rio 2016 and 11,656 athletes at Tokyo 2020; and stabilizes the number of events: 306 events at Rio 2106 and 339 events at Tokyo 2020. For the Winter Games, the IOC recommends 2,900 athletes, 2,000 accredited coaches and athletes' support personnel, and 100 events (2014a). Implementing Recommendation 9 at the Winter Games would have more impact on the number of events than the number of athletes: there were 2,833 athletes and 102 events at Pyeongchang 2018; and 2,897 athletes and 109 events at Beijing 2022. Limiting the number of participants and events allowed at the Olympic Games is an attempt to address concerns about "gigantism" – particularly related to the Summer Games. The IOC worries that the larger the Olympic Games, the more challenging it is to find suitable and willing host cities, as well as about the effects on the experience of the Games.

The IOC's concerns – about including women at the Games and, simultaneously, controlling the size of the Games – are not new. According to Chase (1992), this has been an ongoing debate within the IOC since the earliest decision-making about including women's sports at the Games:

> In the early years, the IOC was constantly striving to reduce the number of participants in the Games [...] primarily for economic reasons. A solution that was often proposed was to eliminate existing female sports and to forbid the entry of new women's sports to the Olympic programme.
>
> *(Chase, 1992: 34)*

To protect the Olympic Games from potential competitors (e.g., the Women's Olympic Games), the IOC explicitly encouraged International Federations to take ownership of women's events in their sports in 1923 (Leigh & Bonin, 1977: 77). By the Seoul 1988 Summer Games, women's events comprised 30.4% of events and women athletes 26.1% of athletes in Seoul – their highest numbers ever. In 1991, "A historic decision was made by the IOC: Any new sport seeking to be included on the Olympic programme had to include women's events" (IOC, 2020a). In order to assess sports more fairly, that is, taking into account less investment in women's sports historically, the IOC established gender differentiated inclusion criteria for new sports.

Specifically, from 1991 to 2004, IFs applying for inclusion at the Summer Games had to demonstrate men's participation in at least 75 countries and on four continents, and women's participation in at least 40 countries and on three continents (IOC, 2017a, *The Olympic Programme Evolution*). For Winter Games' inclusion between 1982 to 2004, IFs had to demonstrate both men's and women's participation in at least 25 countries and on three continents; raised from the 1972 to 1980 expectations for women's participation in at least 20 countries and on two continents (IOC, 2017a, *The Olympic Programme Evolution*). Lenskyj (1990) and Chase (1992) identify these inclusion criteria as one example of the IOC's more recent commitment to gender equality on the Olympic programme, and its recognition of the need to attend to historical differences through a type of affirmative action. The IOC eliminated this requirement beginning with the 2007 *Olympic Charter*, and currently, gender seems to be accounted for primarily in two of five categories into which the assessment criteria are organized: Olympic Proposal; and Institutional Matters (IOC, 2021a, *Olympic Programme Commission*). The IOC claims to have promoted women's sport participation through these requirements: "the IOC has also worked closely with the International Sports Federations (IFs) to stimulate women's involvement in sport through more participation opportunities at the Olympic Games" (IOC, 2020a, *Promotion of women in sport through time*). Notably, in terms of assessment criteria, this is one area in which the IOC has moved away from numbers to criteria that are a little more amorphous; perhaps contributing to frustrations among IFs vying for inclusion on the Olympic programme.

All of this demonstrates the historical context of the IOC's seemingly conflicting goals – formalized in Recommendations 9 and 11 of *Agenda 2020* – to limit (and reduce) the number of athletes and events at the Olympic Games and, at the same time, increase the number of women athletes and women's events. In its attempts to reconcile these conflicting goals, Chase claims, "initiatives to reduce the Olympic programme have interfered with attempts to promote gender equality" (1992: 36). According to Thomas Bach,

> The Olympic Agenda 2020 is like a jigsaw puzzle. Every piece, every recommendation, has the same importance. Only when you put all these 40 pieces together will you see the whole picture. You see progress in ensuring the success of the Olympic Games, progress in safeguarding the Olympic values, and progress in strengthening sport in society.
>
> *(IOC, 2014b)*

Bach explicitly states that no recommendation is more important than the others; however, post-*Agenda 2020* decisions made about the Olympic programme seem to prioritize controlling the size of the Games over meaningful change with respect to gender equality. This is particularly apparent in the IOC's requirement that IF proposals for programme changes will only be approved if they do not require additional athlete quota places. However, the IOC has promoted the idea that it is possible to achieve these conflicting recommendations. For example,

> The Executive Board (EB) Of The International Olympic Committee (IOC) Today Approved The Event Programme For The Olympic Games Tokyo 2020. The Decision Marks A Key Milestone In The Evolution Of The Olympic Programme By Introducing Youth And Urban Innovations, **Significantly Improving Gender Equality, and Reducing The Overall Number of Athletes** Hence Reducing The Games' Footprint.
>
> *(IOC, 2017b,* Tokyo 2020 Event Programme To See Major Boost For Female Participation, Youth and Urban Appeal*, my emphasis).*

As with the London 2012 gender equality achievement claims, the idea of being able to both improve gender equality and reduce the number of athletes at the Games requires close attention. It is in this context that IFs are making decisions about how to "foster gender equality".

What are the numbers?

In the context of the Olympic and Paralympic Games, there are a variety of categories of numbers to assess with respect to gender equality. Specifically, it is necessary to count the number of men and women athletes who participate at the Games, each IF's athlete quota numbers for the Games, the number of events that are available to men and women athletes, and the numbers within specific sports (e.g., number of athletes on teams and the number of teams in a tournament). In this section, I review these categories and offer examples of each.

Number of athletes

The total number of athletes participating at the Summer and Winter Olympic and Paralympic Games has increased at almost every edition of the Games. 11,656 athletes competed at Tokyo 2020 and 2,871 athletes competed at Beijing 2022. The Paralympic Games operate on a much smaller scale than the Olympic Games; 4,403 athletes competed at Tokyo 2020 and 564 athletes competed at Beijing 2022 (IPC, 2021a, 2022). For the first time at the Paris 2024 Summer Olympic Games, there will be a significant decrease in the total number of athletes as the IOC works to limit the number of athletes to 10,500 (due to Recommendation 9 of *Agenda 2020*). The total number of athletes at any edition of the Games results from a combination of factors including athlete quota numbers (detailed in the next section), IF-determined qualification standards for specific events (e.g., required qualifying times in Athletics and Swimming events), and

NOC decision-making about athlete selection processes. In March of 2020, only five months before the Tokyo 2020 Games were originally scheduled, the IOC announced that it would work with the IFs to ensure that each participating NOC would be able to send at least one man athlete and one woman athlete to the Games (IOC, 2021b). In tandem with this announcement, the IOC changed the Opening Ceremony protocol guidelines to allow each NOC to select one man athlete and one woman athlete to carry their flag during the parade of nations (IOC, 2021b). Nations were encouraged, but not required, to select both a man and woman.[1]

Ensuring that each NOC will be able to send at least one man athlete and one woman athlete to all future editions of the Olympic Games is one of the most specific and practical actions the IOC has taken with respect to gender equality. Specifically, a country that did not have any women athletes qualify for the Olympic Games would have the opportunity to identify a woman athlete and – with assistance from the IOC and a specific IF – send that athlete to compete at the Games. The same would be true for countries that did not have any men qualify for the Games. Similarly to the addition of mixed gender events, addressed in chapters 4 and 5, this is an action that is likely to benefit men and women athletes equally. This would be particularly relevant for smaller countries, and also sends a clear message to countries that have previously excluded women from their Olympic teams. There are two main concerns associated with this action: 1. It is unclear how the IOC would work with the IFs to make this happen, especially in the case of Tokyo 2020 because the announcement was made so close in time to the scheduled start of the Games, and because of the IOC's increasingly strict adherence to athlete quotas; and 2. Inclusion of non-qualified athletes at the Games – such as in the relatively widely used "universality" quota places discussed in the next section – is controversial and does not necessarily promote gender equality. For example, facing pressure from IOC President, Jacques Rogge, Saudi Arabia sent 16-year-old judoka, Wojdan Shaherkani, to compete at London 2012; the first ever Saudi woman to compete at the Olympic Games. Shaherkani, a blue belt (two grades below a black belt) in the 78kg weight category, was identified three weeks before the London 2012 Games began, and lasted only one minute and 22 seconds in her first and only contest at the Games (Addley, 2012). There is little question about the value of visibility and representation of women in sport, and on the global stage provided by the Olympic Games; however, when women athletes are unsuccessful to the degree that Shaherkani was, their performances may also be used to promote beliefs about women's unsuitability for sport.

Athlete quota numbers

The IOC determines the total number of athletes at each edition of the Olympic Games and then allocates part of that number to each IF – this is the IF's athlete quota for the Games. This is done by approving (or not) proposals from each IF about the number of events and athletes it would like to have at the next Olympic Games. According to the *Olympic Charter* Rule 46 (2021), IF proposals that require approval of the IOC Executive Board include: "3.1 Establishment of the programme of the Olympic Games in their respective sports and including or deleting disciplines or events"; and "3.2 Establishment of the number of competitors per event and per country, and of the number of teams participating in the Olympic Games". Each IF determines how it will divide its athlete quota among its own events. For example, the International Skating Union (ISU) had an athlete quota of 144 for Figure Skating at Beijing 2022, and five events: men's single skating, women's single skating, pair skating, ice dance, and a team event. The ISU assigned 30 athlete places to each of men's and women's singles, 38 athlete places (19 pairs) to pair skating, and 46 athlete places (23 pairs) to ice dance. Reducing athlete quota numbers is a primary focus of Recommendation 9 (IOC, 2014), and IFs are discouraged from making proposals that require additional athlete quota places. Rather, they are compelled to justify keeping their current number of athlete quota places.

One of the justifications that IFs have offered is the need for athlete quota places to ensure or improve gender equality in their sport at the Olympic Games. For example, World Sailing president, Kim Andersen responded to the IOC's decision about Sailing's programme for Tokyo 2020:

> The IOC Executive Board decision to confirm our 10 medal events for Tokyo 2020, but reduce sailing's quota by 30 sailors is disappointing. [...] Our quota proposal to the IOC would have delivered gender equity at a sport level in 2020.
>
> *(World Sailing, 2017)*

World Sailing's (2017) predicament – trying to "drive the development of the sport in-line with the Olympic Agenda 2020 objectives" – is shared by all IFs. The IOC has not provided any guidance about how to achieve the competing numerical recommendations of *Agenda 2020*.

The combination of gender equality and quotas here is very different from the ways these terms are usually used together. As discussed above, quotas have been identified as one way to achieve gender equality; that is, using a kind of affirmative action to ensure that a specific number of positions within an organization are held by women. It is important to note that the IOC has not, and does not, require IFs to divide their athlete quota numbers equally among men and women athletes, or among men's and women's events. In line with its other commitments to gender equality, the IOC has identified this as a "recommendation" (or a target). Specifically, as part of Recommendation 11, "The IOC to work with the International Federations to achieve 50 per cent female participation in the Olympic Games" (*Agenda 2020*). And, crucially, the IOC has not provided any guidance to IFs about how to work towards "50 per cent female participation" while simultaneously reducing their total athlete quota numbers for Olympic Games held post-*Agenda 2020*.

Athlete quota numbers are comprised of several different kinds of places: qualification places (for athletes and teams who meet an IF's qualifying standards, often organized using continental qualification processes to ensure the most representation of athletes from different continents); host country places (e.g., for Brazilian athletes and teams at Rio 2016); Tripartite Commission invitation places (in individual sports only); and universality places (in Athletics and Swimming). Both the Tripartite Commission invitation and universality places are specially intended to increase the universality of the Summer Olympic Games (there is no equivalent process for the Winter Games). In this sense, universality refers to enabling the greatest number of athletes and countries to participate in all or any of the sports and events on the Summer Olympic programme. The Tripartite Commission is composed of the Association of National Olympic Committees (ANOC), the Association of Summer Olympic International Federations (ASOIF), and the IOC. The objectives of the Commission include

> to manage the allocation procedure for Invitation Places offering the opportunity to NOCs, which have traditionally sent small delegations to the Olympic Games, to be represented at the next edition of the Games. A further objective of the Commission is to contribute to enhancing and reflecting universality by selecting athletes from such NOCs, which are unable to qualify, so that they may have an opportunity to be invited to compete in sports and disciplines for which Invitation Places have been reserved.
> (Olympic Games Tripartite Commission Invitation Places, *2014*).

At Rio 2016, NOCs applied to the Commission for 110 places; these places were part of the overall athlete quota for the Games (*Olympic Games Tripartite Commission Invitation Places*, 2014). The Commission also reallocates some unused qualification places and unused host country places – when NOCs decline or are unable to fill a qualification place – as invitation places.

Only NOCs with "an **average of eight (8) or less [sic] athletes** (athlete quota places) in **individual sports/disciplines** at the last two editions of the Olympic Games (Beijing and London) were eligible for invitation places at Rio 2016" (*Olympic Games Tripartite Commission Invitation Places*, 2014, emphasis in original). NOC-proposed athletes must meet minimum eligibility requirements set by the IF for their sport, have international competition experience in their sport, "an adequate sporting technical level", and have participated in relevant qualifying events (*Olympic Games Tripartite Commission Invitation Places*, 2014). Each of the three parties that form the Tripartite Commission is represented in the allocation criteria: NOC priority; IF priority; and IOC priority. The IOC priority criteria include, among other criteria, universality (inclusion of more NOCs), continental balance, and gender equity; and "The above-mentioned criteria are taken into consideration by the Commission altogether, without any pre-established order or priority or preference" (*Olympic Games Tripartite Commission Invitation Places*, 2014). 101 NOCs were able to apply for invitation places in 16 individual sports (19 disciplines) at Rio 2016. For some sports, the invitation places were identified as being specifically for men athletes and/or for women athletes, and they were "not defined" for other sports. Judo (20) and Shooting (24) had the highest number of invitation places by a large margin, and the places are "not defined" by gender. The next highest number of invitation places was Weightlifting's ten places, six for men athletes and four for women athletes. Overall, there were 31 invitation places defined for men athletes and 28 invitation places defined for women athletes, and 51 invitation places that could be used – by individual NOCs – for men or women athletes without any guidance or requirements from the Tripartite Commission (*Olympic Games Tripartite Commission Invitation Places*, 2014). In many ways, this appears to be a missed opportunity for the IOC (alongside the NOC and IF representatives on the Tripartite Commission) to use invitation places to encourage gender equality in individual sports on the Olympic sport programme. That is, gender equality could be identified as a priority criterion, and the invitation places could be used to facilitate primarily women's participation at the Games.

For the Paralympic Games – Summer and Winter – a Bipartite Commission (composed of the IPC and IFs) has "sought to provide targeted qualification slot allocations in particular sports through the Bipartite Commission Invitation Allocation Method" (IPC, 2021b). These invitation places are included in the overall athlete quota for the Games and are intended to help the IPC and IFs realize the Paralympic Games Guiding Principles: "excellence, diversity, universality, integrity and sustainability" (IPC, 2021b). Among the specified principles that guide the allocation of the Bipartite invitation places (the IPC uses the term "slots") are: "to ensure the representation of athletes with high support needs; to ensure medal events will have sufficient representation for viability; and **to enable greater representation by gender**" (IPC, 2021b, my emphasis). Three of six sports at Beijing 2022 offered Bipartite invitation places: Para Alpine Skiing, Para Nordic Skiing, and Para Snowboard. In both Para Alpine and Nordic Skiing, there were an equal number of men's and women's events (15 each in Alpine and 18 each in Nordic), as well as an equal number of qualification places and Bipartite invitation places available for men skiers and women skiers (IPC, 2021b). In Para Snowboard, there are six men's events and only two women's events – only one classification of women athletes in each of banked slalom and snowboard cross events compared to the three classifications for men athletes in the same two events (IPC, 2021b).[2] There is a corresponding difference in the number of qualification places and Bipartite invitation places for men para snowboarders (70) and the number for women para snowboarders (32) (IPC, 2021b). Along with its Olympic counterpart, the Tripartite Commission, the Paralympic Bipartite Commission has replicated existing gender inequalities in IF-specific athlete quotas, rather than using their invitation places to encourage gender equality. Specifically, when there are fewer qualification places for women, these Commissions typically allocate fewer invitation places as well. In Para Snowboard, there were 17 possible invitation places for men and only

9 possible invitation places for women at Beijing 2022 (IPC, 2021b). If gender equality was elevated to a priority criterion, the invitation places could be used to increase the number of women athletes – relative to men athletes – who participate at the Games.

At the Olympic Summer Games, Universality places are separate from Tripartite Commission invitation places, and they are determined by the two largest Summer Games IFs: Fédération Internationale de Natation (FINA) and World Athletics. Universality places are also used for athletes who have not met the qualifying standards in their event, and are intended to increase the number of NOCs competing in Athletics and Swimming at the Games. According to World Athletics,

> NOCs with no male or female qualified athlete or relay team will be allowed to enter their best male athlete and their best female athlete in one athletic event each, with the exception of the Combined Events [decathlon and heptathlon], 10,000m and 3,000m steeplechase.
>
> (IAAF Qualification System and Entry Standards, *2014*)

Further, "This applies equally to unqualified female entries from an NOC with qualified males, and vice versa" (*IAAF Qualification System and Entry Standards*, 2014). Criteria for selecting the "best" athletes are determined by individual NOCs. Similarly, FINA allowed "NOCs with no swimmers who have achieved an [Olympic Qualifying Time]/'A' Time [...] may enter a maximum of one (1) man *and* one (1) woman" in one individual event each, and

> NOCs with swimmers having achieved an OQT/'A' Time or selected by FINA for an [Olympic Selection Time]/'B' Time only in one (1) gender may also enter one (1) universality swimmer in the other gender, who can participate in one (1) event.
>
> (Qualification System – FINA, *2015*)

Like the Tripartite Commission invitation places, universality places have the potential to be used to promote gender equality; however, NOCs have the option to – they are not required to – identify athletes for these places, which allows some NOCs to continue to exclude women athletes or significantly limit their participation at the Olympic Games. Processes exist for including athletes who are unable to meet the qualifying standards for the Games; it is time that the IOC, IFs, and NOCs prioritize gender equality in these processes.

At the Paralympic Games, some sports such as Boccia, Para Ice Hockey, and Wheelchair Rugby use a "gender-free quota". These athlete quotas have "no restrictions on the number of men and women allowed to compete within an event", or they include places for men athletes, women athletes, and an open category in which men or women athletes can compete (Dean et al., 2021: 5). Dean et al. (2021: 5) found that gender-free quotas have typically resulted in fewer opportunities for women athletes in parasports, "as this strategy does not explicitly protect spots for women". For example, at the Paralympic Winter Games, Para Ice Hockey uses a predominantly gender-free quota. At Beijing 2022, eight teams competed in the Para Ice Hockey tournament, and the total athlete quota was designated as eight female and 136 gender free (IPC, 2021b). Each National Paralympic Committee (NPC) was able to "enter a maximum of one (1) team comprised of either seventeen (17) eligible male athletes or eighteen (18) eligible athletes of whom a minimum of one (1) athlete must be female" (IPC, 2021b). In spite of the "gender-free" quota, the expectation is clearly that the vast majority of athletes on Para Ice Hockey teams are men. According to Bundon (*Paralympic Games left behind in the race towards gender equality*, 2022),

> Although women are 'eligible' to compete, few make the team or a single woman is sent to say they met the quota. For example, looking through the history of para ice hockey (sled hockey), it is listed as mixed but we have only identified two countries that have ever sent a woman, and it's very unclear if they actually got any playing time.

In this case, it seems that having an athlete quota composed of gender-free places and a (very small) number of "female" places actually reinforces the idea that non-female places are for male athletes.

Dean et al. (2021: 5) identified a similar situation in Wheelchair Rugby, which "has a gender-free quota yet has one of the lowest participation rates from women across the Paralympic Movement with women accounting for only 2% of all wheelchair rugby athletes". They emphasize that "it is also important to consider the ways in which gender ideologies, in addition to athlete quotas, influence women's involvement within traditionally masculine sporting contexts, like wheelchair ruby" (Dean et al., 2021: 5). Some of the rules-based elements of Para Ice Hockey and Wheelchair Rugby that bolster their cultures as hypermasculine parasports that are more appropriate for men athletes are discussed in the next chapter. Ultimately, what the Paralympic use of gender-free quotas demonstrates is that these quotas are, more often than not, filled by men athletes. As discussed in chapter 4, this aligns with the historical participation in "open" events at the Olympic Games. Open events in Luge and Sailing have traditionally been contested exclusively by men athletes, even though women athletes have not been excluded from participating. It is also important to examine the ways that a designation such as "gender-free" is understood – and used – by NOCs and IFs. For example, is it possible that it leads to a kind of gender-blind sexism (like the colour-blind racism perpetuated by White people claiming they "don't see colour")? Or, at the least, to leaving the status quo unchallenged?

Athlete quota numbers are highly contested between IFs and the IOC, and among IFs. Like the number of events (discussed in the next section), each IF wants to have the highest possible number of athlete quota places at the Games. Consistently, at recent editions of the Summer and Winter Games, when there is a difference in the number of athlete quota places for men and women in an event, the number is always higher for men athletes. This is often related to the number of men's events and women's events. That is, when there are more events for men athletes in a sport, there are often proportionally more places for men athletes in that sport. For example, at Rio 2016, the athlete quota for Canoe/Kayak Sprint was 158 men paddlers and 88 women paddlers. This reflected the fact that men participated in eight events and women in only four events at Rio 2016; the difference of 70 athletes is accounted for by 20 athletes in the men's K2 1000m, 13 athletes in each of the C1 100m and 200m, and 24 athletes in the 1000m – all events scheduled only for men at Rio 2016 (*Qualification System – ICF*, 2014). When men and women paddlers competed in the same six events at Tokyo 2020 (with one exception, a K1 1,000m for men and 500m for women), the athlete quota numbers were the same: 123 men and 123 women (*Qualification System – ICF*, 2019). The IOC has confirmed the politics of allocating athlete quota numbers. Athlete quota numbers for Weightlifting and Boxing at the Paris 2024 Summer Games were reduced more than any other sports on the programme, and the IOC explained that this was due, in the case of Weightlifting, to "its strong concerns with regard to the governance of the International Weightlifting Federation (IWF) and the doping history of the sport"; and, in the case of Boxing, to "the ongoing concerns about the International Boxing Association (AIBA)" (IOC, 2020c).

Perhaps surprisingly, newer sports on the Olympic programme have not necessarily been more gender equal in terms of athlete quota numbers than existing sports. BMX Cycling racing events were added to the Summer Olympic sport programme at Beijing 2008, and at Rio 2016, there were 32 athlete quota places for men BMX riders and only 16 for women BMX riders. It was not until Tokyo 2020 that the Union Cycliste Internationale (UCI) allocated an equal number of athlete quota places to men and women BMX riders; 24 for men and 24 for women. The concerning decision to redistribute athlete quota places among men and women athletes – that is, eliminating athlete quota places previously designated for men and designating them for women – within sports and disciplines is discussed below. Similar to BMX racing, when the Fédération Internationale de Ski (FIS) added the halfpipe and slopestyle events to Freestyle Skiing at the Sochi 2014 Winter Games, each had an athlete quota of 30 men skiers and 24 women skiers. At Beijing 2022, the FIS allocated 25 athlete quota places for both men and women skiers in the halfpipe events, and 30 athlete quota places for both men and women skiers in the slopestyle and big air events (the two events shared an athlete quota). Most importantly, these numbers show that the newer, youth-focused, "cool" events the IOC has been so keen to add to the Olympic programme are not necessarily gender equal. Whether or not they are included in ways that are gender equal is determined by IF-level decision-making about, in part, how to allocate athlete quota numbers to these new events. These decisions are further complicated by the IOC's messaging that new events will only be approved if they do not require additions to an IF's athlete quota numbers.

Number of events

The sport programme–related recommendations of *Agenda 2020* will likely result in less change to the number of events than the number of athletes at each edition of the Games. Specifically, Recommendation 9 calls for 310 events at the Summer Games and 100 events at the Winter Games; fewer events than the most recent Tokyo 2020 (339 events) and Beijing 2022 Games (109). Each IF wants to have the highest number of events possible on the Olympic programme for their sport – more events mean more medals and more opportunities for media coverage. According to Pape (2020: 98),

> [...] the IFs were 'a little prejudiced' in wanting to be 'represented on the Programme with as many events as possible' (M9, 5). Expanding the number of women's sports and events was a cause the IFs were willing to pursue: It delivered them an increased presence at the Olympic Games without compromising their own gendered organizational logics.

Many IFs have viewed adding women's events as one way to increase their presence at the Olympic Games without necessarily being committed to gender equality – or even gender parity – in any meaningful way, i.e., in terms of the organization and operation of their sport.

Even with the consistent addition of women's events by many IFs, it will not be until Paris 2024 that the Summer Olympic Games' programme will feature an equal number of men's and women's events (*Official Programme of the Olympic Games Paris 2024*, 2020). Current differences in the number of men's events and women's events at the Summer Games are largely accounted for by gender exclusive sports, and gender exclusive disciplines and events within a sport. Notably, there will continue to be gender exclusive events at Paris 2024, but for the first time, there will be an equal number of events for men only and for women only. At the Olympic Summer Games, Artistic Swimming and Rhythmic Gymnastics – both added in Los Angeles 1984 – are women-only sports. At the Winter Games, Nordic Combined remains the only Olympic sport for men only. At the Paralympic Games, both 5-a-side and 7-a-side Football (the latter was not included at Tokyo 2020) have been men-only sports. When the IOC celebrated that, with the inclusion of women's events in Boxing, women competed in all sports on the Olympic programme at London 2012, they did not identify that there are sports in which only women compete. They also did not address the fact that women's inclusion in Boxing, as in other sports at the Games, was not equal in terms of the number of women athletes relative to men athletes or their conditions of participation.

Many sports are composed of one or more disciplines, such as Cycling, which contains four disciplines at the Olympic Games: BMX, Mountain, Road, and Track. There are two Wrestling disciplines included on the Olympic programme, and women wrestlers only compete in Freestyle Wrestling, while men wrestlers compete in both Freestyle and Greco Roman Wrestling. Until Tokyo 2020, the International Canoe Federation (ICF) determined that women paddlers competed only in Kayak events – Sprint and Slalom – while men paddlers competed in both Canoe and Kayak events. For the first time at Tokyo 2020, and after much athlete advocacy, women paddlers competed in C1 200m and C2 500m races, races that have long been part of the women's programme at ICF World Championships. There are no disciplines for women only in any sport at either the Summer or Winter Olympic Games.

Within sports and disciplines, there are many events in which only men have historically competed. At the Summer Olympic Games these include a 50km race walk in Athletics (which has been replaced with a to be determined mixed gender race walk event at Paris 2024); two more apparatuses in Artistic Gymnastics (men and women compete on both the floor exercise and vault, while only women compete on the balance beam and uneven parallel bars, and only men compete on the horizontal bar, parallel bars, pommel horse, and rings); additional weight categories in Boxing, Weightlifting, and Wrestling; and a one-person heavyweight dinghy (Finn class) in Sailing. At the Winter Olympic Games, only men compete in the four-man Bobsled and Luge doubles events (after adding women's doubles to the World Cup season in 2021–2022, the International Luge Federation (FIL) has proposed its inclusion at Milan-Cortina 2026). Multiple athletes compete in each of these events, which has resulted in consistently more men athletes than women athletes at the Olympic Games. The disparity in the number of men's and women's events has been the most significant barrier to achieving gender parity in the number of athletes at the Olympic Games.

At the Paralympic Games, much of the focus on gender parity has been directed to events being added to the sport programme. According to Dean et al. (2021: 5), the IPC has required gender balance as a "criterion for petitioning sports". New sports added to the Summer Paralympic Games for Rio 2016 (Triathlon and Canoe Sprint) and Tokyo 2020 (Badminton and Taekwondo) all have an equal number of events and athlete quota places for men and women para athletes (Dean et al., 2021). The expectation that new sports and events are gender balanced before they are included on the Paralympic sport programme is evidence of greater emphasis on gender equality:

> The addition of these events to the Paralympic Games illustrates that the IPC is willing to create some added opportunities for women within the Paralympic Movement. Unfortunately, the requirement of gender balance has not been applied to parasports already on the program as there are still events within the Paralympics that are only available to men.
>
> *(Dean et al., 2021: 5)*

Gender equality cannot be an expectation only for new sports and events to be included at the Olympic and Paralympic Games. A genuine commitment to gender equality requires a review of all existing sports and events, both in terms of their numbers and conditions of participation.

Adding women's sports and events is crucial to achieving gender equality at both the Olympic and Paralympic Games. However, McLachlan (2016) identifies the need to problematize the "inclusion narratives" of the Olympic Games. The typical focus of sport historians on questions such as, "what were the major forces that led to the inclusion of [a specific event] for women [at the Olympic Games]?" are necessarily limiting: "A problem with this is that the 'historic moment' of the inclusion of a specific event (usually for women) is seen as an endpoint, it is often implied in such narratives that getting in, is enough" (McLachlan, 2016: 471). The IOC's promotion of similar kinds of inclusion narratives, such as those about women's Boxing at London 2012 and women's Ski Jumping at Sochi 2014, serves the same purpose. That is, the IOC effectively maintains the existing gender inequalities – qualitative and quantitative – on the Olympic programme by leaving them unchallenged. Instead, the focus is entirely on the "historic moment of inclusion", even when that inclusion is thoroughly unequal. In the case of Boxing, this meant women boxers' inclusion at London 2012 in three weight categories compared to the ten weight categories available to men boxers. This was the case even though the International Boxing Association (IBA) recognizes ten weight categories for Elite women boxers. Further, the athlete quota for women's boxing was 36 athletes (12 athletes per weight category) compared to 250 men boxers (25 athletes per weight category). Inclusion narratives, such as the IOC's numbers-focused claims about gender equality achievements at the Olympic Games, warrant close examination to determine what is actually happening at the Games, and to continue the discussion about gender equality beyond the "moment of inclusion".

Within sport number differences

A final, numerical point of scrutiny of sports on the Olympic programme is distinct for each of the team sports and individual sports. In June 2016, the IOC announced that it had approved five sports proposed by the Tokyo Organizing Committee of the Olympic and Paralympic Games (TOCOG), "The package [of new sports] promotes **gender equality, with each of the five sports having equal numbers of teams for men and women** [...]" (IOC, 2016c, my emphasis). With this specific celebration – that the sports would each have an equal number of men's and women's teams – the IOC called attention to the existing differences in the number of teams in other sports. For example, at the most recent Summer Olympic Games (Rio 2016 and Tokyo 2020), 16 men's teams and 12 women's teams competed in the Football tournament; and 12 men's teams and 10 women's teams (two more teams than Rio 2016) competed in the Water Polo tournament. At the most recent Winter Olympic Games (Pyeongchang 2018 and Beijing 2022), 12 men's teams and 10 women's teams (two more than Pyeongchang 2018) competed in the Ice Hockey tournament. There are not only fewer women's teams in Ice Hockey, but there are also fewer women players on each team – 23 women compared to 25 men. Notably, in the IOC's claim about equal numbers of men's and women's teams in the five new sports for Tokyo 2020, they failed to acknowledge one significant difference. Based on the rules of the World Baseball Softball Confederation (WBSC), there were 24 athletes on each of the six men's Baseball teams and only 15 athletes on each of the six women's Softball teams at Tokyo 2020; resulting in places for 54 more men athletes than women athletes at the Games.

In individual sports, the difference may be in the number of athletes included in a relay or team event. For example, at Rio 2016 and Tokyo 2020, the UCI determined that each NOC would be represented by three men cyclists in the men's team sprint event, and only two women cyclists in the women's team sprint event in Track Cycling. Or, the difference may be in the ways that men and women athletes compete. At the same Summer Games, men divers in all four Diving events (individual and synchronized 3m springboard and 10m platform) performed six dives in each round of the competition, while women divers performed only five dives in each round. Women mountain bikers ride six laps of the designated course, while men mountain bikers ride seven laps. In some sports, related to the number of athletes in each event, women athletes compete fewer times during their participation at the Games. In Boxing, women boxers have competed only in a round of 16, quarter-finals, semi-finals, and finals. Because there are so many more men boxers in the men's tournament, men also compete in a round of 32, which means they have five opportunities to compete, while women boxers have only four. Similarly, in BMX Racing at Rio 2016, 32 men BMX riders had the potential to compete in four rounds – seedings, quarter-finals and semi-finals (each composed of three runs), and finals, while 16 women BMX riders had only three rounds of competition, with no quarter-finals. When the athlete quota numbers were equalized for Tokyo 2020, both men and women BMX riders had the potential to compete in three rounds – quarter-finals, semi-finals, and finals. This further demonstrates the ways that the categories of numbers are interdependent.

ALL the numbers

The number of numbers associated with gender equality and the Games can seem overwhelming, and the IOC (and IFs) often reports about these numbers in ways that are self-serving and not always accurate (or, at least, telling the full story). Consistently, at both the Olympic and Paralympic Games, when there has been a difference in the numbers for men and women, men have always had more – a higher number of athletes, athlete quota places, events, athletes on teams, and teams in tournaments. And, the numbers are highly contested and political; each IF wants to have the greatest possible representation in all of the numbers on the Olympic and Paralympic sport programmes, and the IOC wants to reward sports and events that are youth-focused, "urban" (at the Summer Games), and it claims, gender equal (IOC, 2020c). As the previous sections demonstrate, the categories of numbers are interconnected and largely interdependent. A change to one category of numbers has consequences for most of the other categories. The consequences of changes to the total athlete quota numbers for the Olympic Games, and their relationship to gender equality, are the focus of the next section.

Managing conflicting numerical recommendations – at the expense of the athletes

In December 2020, the IOC approved the sport programme and athlete quota numbers for the Paris 2024 Summer Games, and highlighted specific, numbers-focused achievements including: "Exactly 50 per cent male and female participation"; "Reduction in the overall athlete quota (including all new sports) to exactly 10,500"; and "Reduction in the overall number of events, with a final programme of 329 events" (IOC, 2020c). According to the IOC, there will be 592 fewer athlete quota places at Paris 2024 than at Tokyo 2020: "The reduction across the 28 sports has been proportionate and focused on those sports that can best absorb the reduction, whilst maintaining the universality of the Games" (IOC, 2020c). IFs, then, have been tasked with – for the most part – allocating an equal number of quota places to men and women athletes in the name of gender equality, while also decreasing the total number of athletes competing in their sport (in the name of reducing "the overall size and complexity of the Games" (IOC, 2020c)). Further complicating this task is the IOC's decision to reject all IF proposals for additional events at Paris 2024 (41 in total), and reduce the total number of events to 329 (ten fewer events than at Tokyo 2020) (IOC, 2020c). There will be eight new events at Paris 2024, which were only approved because they "replac[e] existing events, in each case to ensure no increases in event numbers" (IOC, 2020c). The celebratory tone of this announcement, and the softer language of "reduction", "replacement", and "transfer", belie the fact that these are decisions that eliminate athlete places and events. In elite sport, when athletes often identify at a very young age the Olympic Games they will strive to qualify for, this means fewer – and, in the case of eliminated events, no – opportunities to participate at those Games. It is hard to understand this as a "win" for gender equality.

The reality of the Olympic context of conflicting numerical *Agenda 2020* recommendations – Recommendation 9 to reduce the size of the Games and Recommendation 11 to "foster gender equality" – is one in which a lot of athletes lose. Of particular concern is the now common practice among IFs of eliminating places for men athletes and men's events to add places for women athletes and women's events. This is a significant shift from the IOC and IFs' historical approach, described by Pape (2020: 96), when "Extensive bureaucratic hurdles to the expansion of women's sport were underpinned by concern regarding the overall size of the program ('gigantism') and resistance to reducing men's competition opportunities". Bach's claim that "Every piece, every recommendation [of *Agenda 2020*], has the same importance" (IOC, 2014b) is not supported by the numbers. In strictly adhering to the 10,500 athlete quota "recommendation" for Paris 2024, the IOC has prioritized concerns about the overall size of the Games over other programme-related recommendations, and especially, gender equality. IFs are in a nearly impossible situation with respect to increasing the number of opportunities for women in their sport at the Games; at least in ways that most would recognize as gender equality.

Whether gender equality is understood more broadly – "it's about equal status! Women and men can fully realize their fundamental rights and have equal opportunities and rights" – or in exclusively numerical terms – "The goal is to reach a balanced ration of women and men (ideally, 50/50) in terms of representation and participation at all levels" – eliminating opportunities for men in order to add opportunities for women is *not* gender equality (Gender Wire, UNESCO, 2015). It is also not an unanticipated approach to attempting to resolve the conflicting numerical recommendations of *Agenda* 2020. Donnelly and Donnelly (2013: 30) warned against this approach following the London 2012 Summer Games:

> Although men's events have already been cut in order to add new women's events (e.g., Boxing dropped one men's weight category in order to add three women's weight categories), and women's positions have been cut in order to manage the total number of athletes (e.g., women's positions were reduced from three to two per country in Cycling-Mountain at the London 2012 Olympics, while men still maintained three riders per country), it should be remembered that men and women athletes are not the one's responsible for 'gigantism' or for gender inequality at the Olympics, and should not be the ones to suffer through resolving one problem by creating another. If achieving gender equality means increasing the size of the Olympic Programme, at least temporarily, so be it.

However, to date, the IOC has not provided any guidance to IFs about how to effectively and fairly manage their numbers to achieve both overall reductions and increase opportunities for women athletes.

In the absence of any IOC guidance, and limited by the IOC's refusal to add athlete quota places or events to the sport programme, many IFs have reduced their athlete quota numbers for men in order to increase the numbers for women, and have replaced men's events with women's events (and sometimes mixed gender events). This trend became apparent at the Rio 2016 Summer Games: World Rowing eliminated 22 places for men rowers and added 22 places for women rowers; World Sailing eliminated 20 places for men sailors and added 20 places for women sailors; and United World Wrestling (UWW) eliminated 30 places for men wrestlers and added 40 places for women wrestlers. In terms of events, World Sailing eliminated one men's event and one women's event, and added a new women's event and a mixed gender event; and UWW eliminated two men's weight categories and added two women's weight categories. IFs have not only continued to make these decisions, but the reassignment of athlete places and events from men to women also increased dramatically for Tokyo 2020 and affected athletes in even more sports.

IFs consistently justify their decisions in terms of gender equality or, more broadly, achieving the goals of *Agenda 2020*. When the International Shooting Sport Federation (ISSF) announced – in a lengthy press release – its intention to eliminate three men's events for Tokyo 2020 (50m rifle prone, 50m pistol, double trap), it explained that the decision was "in response to the requirements of the International Olympic Committee's Agenda 2020":

> The first decision of the Ad-Hoc Committee [appointed by the president to prepare recommendations for achieving gender equality in Shooting] was to preserve discipline parity and retain 15 Olympic shooting events – 5 Rifle, 5 Pistol, 5 Shotgun. Each of the three disciplines currently has three men's events and two women's events in the Olympic program. The Committee decided that the best way to achieve gender equality was to convert one men's event in each discipline to a mixed gender team event.
>
> *(ISSF, 2017)*

As a result of this decision, athletes competing in the three eliminated events (which were all for men only) had no opportunity to participate at Tokyo 2020. Further, as discussed in chapter 5, the mixed-gender team events are contested by athletes who have already qualified for the Games in a single-gender event. This maintains the number of medal events in Shooting without adding (or even replacing) any athlete places. According to the ISSF, these "difficult, emotional and courageous decisions" were made by people who "tried to act in the best interests of future generations in our sport while emphasizing the priority of keeping Shooting in the Olympic Games" (ISSF, 2017). This suggests that the ISSF interprets not adhering to the IOC's commitment to gender equality as having the potential to jeopardize Shooting's place on the Olympic programme.

Preserving their place – and athlete quota places and events – at the Olympic Games is the top priority for IFs, and this informs how they respond to the IOC's recommendations, such as those in *Agenda 2020*. In his first speech after being elected president of the ICF, Thomas Konietzo, exemplified this:

> In Paris organisers wanted to introduce extreme sports, so to do that we had to reduce some disciplines. If we talk about [the inclusion of] baseball-softball with a view to Los Angeles 2028, there would be the need for 100 quotas which would be taken away from other sports that are not appealing. For this reason I am telling you that we have to evolve. We have to develop our federation and the goal of the new Board has to be to keep our quotas. We have to be ready to [sic] the fact the IOC might ask us to

> introduce some changes, as has happened in other federations. We cannot lose our quotas and we cannot lose our medals, so we have to change.
>
> *(in Rowbottom, 2021)*

Notably, Konietzo also identified the impact these changes have on athletes: "And we also have to think a lot about our athletes. If someone comes in that means we have to scratch other disciplines and athletes are affected by our decisions" (in Rowbottom, 2021). Conversely, as discussed below, the IOC consistently presents a solely positive story about changes that are made to the Olympic programme.

According to Gillen (2019), at Tokyo 2020, the number of weight categories for men boxers was reduced from ten to eight, and the number of weight categories for women boxers increased from three to five. "This follows the IOC's commitment to balance the number of female and male athletes competing at the Games" (Gillen, 2019). And, in preparation for Paris 2024, World Athletics has eliminated the men's 50km racewalk event. While racewalkers advocated for the inclusion of a women's 50km event at the Games, the IOC determined that the race would be replaced by a mixed-gender racewalk team event, the details of which had not yet been determined: "Achieving gender parity while not increasing the number of athletic events were key considerations, the IOC said" (Gallagher, 2021). The IOC also frames these decisions in terms of gender equality. In the press release announcing approval of the Tokyo 2020 sport programme, the IOC celebrated "Today's decision is a significant step towards achieving the 50 per cent gender balance at the Olympic Games in both athletes and events, as clearly stated by Olympic Agenda 2020" (IOC, 2017b). In a list of new events, the IOC explicitly identified when IFs had eliminated numbers from men to add to women. In the case of Boxing, Canoe, and Rowing, the IOC indicated that there had been a "Transfer of [# of] men's events to [# of] women's events" – two, three, and one respectively. Similarly for athlete quota numbers, the IOC detailed that in the case of Boxing, there was a "Transfer of 44 athletes from men to women", and that in a number of sports (e.g., Canoe, BMX Racing), there was a "Transfer of [# of] athletes to reach gender balance" (IOC, 2017b). In other sports (e.g., Judo, Rowing, Weightlifting), they claimed there was a "Reduction of [# of] athletes and reach gender balance" (IOC, 2017b), which suggests that the IOC-imposed athlete quota number reductions were applied almost exclusively to men athletes in these sports.

Not only has the IOC allowed this to happen – by approving the proposed changes from IFs and the overall Olympic programme – it also promotes these decisions without comment about what they mean for gender equality (in its fullest sense) at the Olympic Games. Specifically, in press releases (and other public announcements), the IOC has celebrated IFs that have achieved gender-balanced event numbers and/or gender-balanced athlete quotas, no matter how they have accomplished that balance. For example, highlighting that, at Tokyo 2020,

> Four new International Federations (IFs) will move to gender-balanced in events for the first time (Canoe, Rowing, Shooting and Weightlifting). In terms of athletes, six IFs will move to gender balance for the first time (Canoe, Judo, Rowing, Sailing, Shooting and Weightlifting). At discipline level, gender balance is achieved in BMX Racing, Mountain Bike and Freestyle Wrestling.
>
> *(IOC, 2017b)*

And, advertising that "Athletics, boxing and cycling will reach full gender equality for the first time ever at Paris 2024, meaning 28 out of 32 sports on the Paris 2024 programme will be fully gender balanced" (IOC, 2020c). According to UN Women, a partner organization of the IOC since 2012, gender equality

> refers to the equal rights, responsibilities and opportunities of women and men and girls and boys. [...] **Gender equality implies that the interests, needs and priorities of both women and men are taken into consideration, recognizing the diversity of different groups of women and men. Gender equality is not a women's issue but should concern and fully engage men as well as women.**
>
> *(Gender Equality Glossary, UN Women, my emphasis)*

There is no acknowledgement on the part of the IOC that gender equality "is not [only] a women's issue" when it allows IFs to cut men's athlete quota places and events to add women's athlete quota places and events. Despite its claims to use an "'athletes-first' approach" (IOC, 2020c), the IOC is solely responsible for creating a situation in which athletes – and men athletes in particular – bear the burden of achieving recommendations when athletes had nothing to do with creating the problems those recommendations attempt to solve.

Some American high schools and universities have tried to make similar choices to those being made by IFs, i.e., to cut men's teams rather than add women's teams at their institutions, and justify their decisions as a result of "gender equality" in the form of Title IX. Title IX is the legislation that prohibits gender-based discrimination in federally funded education programs, and which had an overwhelmingly positive influence on women's and girls' sport participation numbers in the United States after it was passed in 1972. Unlike the IOC, the Office of Civil Rights (OCR) that oversees Title IX compliance has issued guidance about this situation:

> OCR hereby clarifies that nothing in Title IX requires the cutting or reduction of teams in order to demonstrate compliance with Title IX, and that the elimination of teams is a disfavored practice. Because the elimination of teams diminishes opportunities for students who are interested in participating in athletics instead of enhancing opportunities for students who have suffered from discrimination, it is contrary to the spirit of Title IX.
>
> *(Dear Colleague letter, 2003)*

The IOC has effectively created a "zero sum game" requiring that IFs work within the constraints of a set, and inflexible, athlete quota number for the Games. The IOC must provide guidance – and flexibility – for IFs to make decisions that serve the interests of all athletes. Further, for the IOC's commitment to gender equality to be meaningful, they need to recognize that they are fostering potential backlash to gender equality initiatives, and specifically to increasing the number of women athletes and women's events at the Games, by using them as a "convenient scapegoat" to explain the elimination of athlete quota places and events on the sport programme (Walton, 2003).[3] Increasing opportunities for women athletes at the Games should not be associated with eliminating opportunities for men athletes at the Games. This is not gender equality, and it foments unnecessary resentment and conflict among men and women athletes.

Conclusion

Focusing on the numbers associated with the Olympic programme is a way to assess the IOC on its own terms. The IOC has clearly demonstrated – without ever offering a specific definition – that its gender equality commitment is actually about gender parity. When there are an equal number of men and women athletes and men's and women's events approved for the sport programme, the IOC will claim it has achieved gender equality (or, more commonly, gender balance). Even when the number of men and women athletes is not equal, the IOC has celebrated achieving gender balance. According to the IOC (2020c),

> The Olympic Games Tokyo 2020 next year will be the first gender equal Olympic Games, with an overall 48.8 per cent female participation, which will be further increased at Paris 2024, reaching the exact same number of male and female athletes for the first time in Olympic history.

Not only is the IOC's statement confusing – by suggesting that Tokyo 2020 will be gender equal but not yet have "the exact same number of male and female athletes" – it minimizes the inequality in the number of athletes. In the same press release, the IOC (2020c) reported that there were 11,092 athletes at Tokyo 2020; 1.2% of that total is 133 athletes. There were 133 more men athletes than women athletes at Tokyo 2020. That is more than the total athlete quota numbers for some sports at the Summer Games. This is another reminder that the IOC's claims about numbers and gender equality need to be carefully examined.

Further, when the IOC focuses exclusively on numbers, and even then, exclusively on the number of athletes and events, the full story of gender parity – or the lack thereof – at the Olympic Games is obscured. All of the categories of numbers – athletes, athlete quota numbers, events, and sport-specific numbers – offer important information about how gender equality informs IF and IOC decision-making about the Olympic programme. What is revealed is a prioritizing of men over women, and an even more consistent prioritizing of the overall size of the Games over gender equality. The IOC's lack of guidance to IFs about how to achieve the conflicting numerical recommendations of Agenda 2020 has created a situation in which men and women athletes (and men's and women's events) are pitted against each other, vying for a fixed number of places on the sport programme. Doing so jeopardizes movement towards gender equality in two main ways. First, by eliminating from men to add for women, which does not meet any definition of gender equality. Second, when new opportunities for women athletes and women's events at the Games are promoted as being the result of eliminating opportunities for men athletes and men's events, those new opportunities are understood in terms of loss, and negative consequences. This cannot engender positive feelings about gender equality.

Finally, almost entirely missing from the IOC's numbers-focused commitment to gender equality is attention to the different ways that men athletes and women athletes are required to participate in many sports on the Olympic programme at both the Summer and Winter Games. These gender-based differences in the conditions of participation are the focus of the following chapter.

Notes

1 At most Olympic Games, NOCs' ability to select both a man athlete and woman athlete to carry their flag would be a more visible aspect of the IOC's commitment to gender equality. Unfortunately at Tokyo 2020 many athletes, due to COVID restrictions, were not able to take part in the parade of nations during the Opening Ceremonies, which did not offer a good sense of how many nations would take advantage of this option. What was visible in Tokyo was the IOC's decision to have both a man and a woman athlete take the Olympic Oath. The language of the Oath was updated to include "without any form of discrimination".

2 Elite para snowboarders appealed the IPC's decision to eliminate the women's LL1 snowboard cross and banked slalom events and only include LL2 classification events at Beijing 2022. The athletes' letter – signed by 45 athletes from 12 countries – read, in part,

> Since 2014, the Paralympic Movement has aimed to include women with leg impairments in Winter Paralympic Games. We believe having only one category competing in Beijing doesn't represent inclusion in our sport. We, as women competitors, are united in promoting our sport. We believe it would be unfair to exclude women with the highest degree of impairment from the most important event.
>
> (in Burke, 2021)

Attempting to negotiate among principles, event numbers, and athlete quota numbers is a challenge for IFs at both the Olympic and Paralympic Games.

3 In a study of media reports about Title IX and wrestling, Walton (2003: 22) found that

> Title IX has been a convenient scapegoat for athletic departments to point to when cutting men's teams rather than address the escalating expenditures in men's basketball and football. This has the double effect of decreasing public support for Title IX and allowing schools to continue discriminatory spending within their athletic departments – while continuing to cut men's wrestling teams.

References

Addley, Esther (3 August 2012). Saudi Arabia's judoka strikes blow for women's rights at Olympics. *The Guardian*. https://www.theguardian.com/sport/london-2012-olympics-blog/2012/aug/03/saudi-wojdan-shaherkani-women-olympics. Retrieved: 10 September, 2012.

Adriaanse, Johanna A. (2017). Quotas to accelerate gender equity in sport leadership: Do they work? In Laura J. Burton & Sarah Leberman (Eds.), *Women in Sport and Leadership: Research and Practice for Change* (pp. 83–97). Abingdon: Routledge.

Burke, Patrick (5 December 2021). Para snowboarders call on IPC to allow women's LL1 athletes to compete at Beijing 2022. https://www.insidethegames.biz/articles/1116416/para-snowboard-ll1-beijing-2022. Retrieved: 15 December, 2021.

Chase, Laura F. (1992). A policy analysis of gender inequality within the Olympic movement. In Robert K. Barney & Klaus V. Meier (Eds.), *Proceedings: First International Symposium for Olympic Research* (pp. 28–39). London, ON: International Centre for Olympic Studies.

Dean, Nikolaus A., Andrea Bundon, P. David Howe & Natalie Abele (2021). Gender parity, false starts, and promising practices in the Paralympic movement. *Sociology of Sport Journal* (Ahead of print). https://doi.org/10.1123/ssj.2021-0030

Dear Colleague letter from Assistant Secretary for Civil Rights Gerald Reynolds (11 July 2003). Further clarification of intercollegiate athletics policy guidance regarding Title IX compliance. United States Department of Education, Office for Civil Rights.

Donnelly, Peter & Michele K. Donnelly (2013). *The London 2012 Olympics: A Gender Equality Audit*. Centre for Policy Studies Research Report. Toronto: Centre for Sport Policy Studies, Faculty of Kinesiology and Physical Education, University of Toronto.

Gallagher, Chris (6 August 2021). Athletics-walkers slam decision to scrap 50km race. https://www.reuters.com/lifestyle/sports/athletics-walkers-slam-decision-scrap-50km-race-2021-08-06/. Retrieved: 9 August, 2021.

Gillen, Nancy (3 October 2019). Kremlev calls for 10 Olympic weight divisions for female boxers. https://www.insidethegames.biz/articles/1085519/kremlev-ten-olympic-weight-divisions. Retrieved: 3 November, 2019.

Houghton, Emily J., Lindsay Pieper & Maureen Smith. (2018). *Women in the 2018 Olympic and Paralympic Winter Games: An Analysis of Participation, Leadership, and Media Coverage*. New York: Women's Sports Foundation.

Institut National de la Statistique et des Études Économiques (n.d.). Parity and equality between women and men. https://www.insee.fr/en/metadonnees/definition/c1296. Retrieved: 14 January, 2020.

International Association of Athletics Federations (April 2014). Qualification system and entry standards (Games of the XXXI Olympiad Rio 2016).

IOC (2014a). *Olympic Agenda 2020: 20 +20 Recommendations*. Lausanne: International Olympic Committee.

IOC (7 December 2014b). 127th IOC Session opens in Monaco – President Bach delivers keynote speech. https://olympics.com/ioc/news/127th-ioc-session-opens-in-monaco-president-bach-delivers-keynote-speech. Retrieved: 3 February, 2018.

IOC (21 August 2015). IOC achieves full gender equality for the first time, at the Youth Olympic Games Buenos Aires 2018. https://olympics.com/ioc/news/ioc-achieves-full-gender-equality-for-the-first-time-at-the-youth-olympic-games-buenos-aires-2018-1. Retrieved: 3 February, 2018.

IOC (June 2016a). Factsheet – Women in the Olympic Movement. https://stillmed.olympics.com/media/Documents/Olympic-Movement/Factsheets/Women-in-the-Olympic-Movement.pdf

IOC (1 June 2016b). IOC executive board supports Tokyo 2020 package of new sports for IOC session. https://olympics.com/ioc/news/ioc-executive-board-supports-tokyo-2020-package-of-new-sports-for-ioc-session. Retrieved: 15 June, 2016.

IOC (2017a). The Olympic programme evolution. Olympic Studies Centre. https://library.olympics.com/Default/doc/SYRACUSE/174657/the-olympic-programme-evolution-the-olympic-studies-centre?_lg=en-GB

IOC (9 June 2017b). Tokyo 2020 event programme to see major boost for female participation, youth and urban appeal. https://olympics.com/ioc/news/tokyo-2020-event-programme-to-see-major-boost-for-female-participation-youth-and-urban-appeal. Retrieved: 3 February, 2018.

IOC (2020a). Key dates in the history of women in the Olympic Movement. https://www.olympic.org/women-in-sport/background/key-dates. Retrieved: July 9, 2020.

IOC (28 January 2020b). Mixed events enrich the Winter Games Programme. https://www.olympic.org/news/mixed-events-enrich-the-winter-games-programme. Retrieved: 21 February, 2021.

IOC (7 December 2020c). Gender equality and youth at the heart of the Paris 2024 Olympic Sports Programme. https://www.olympic.org/news/gender-equality-and-youth-at-the-heart-of-the-paris-2024-olympic-sports-programme. Retrieved: 21 February, 2021.

IOC (2021a). Olympic Programme Commission. https://olympics.com/ioc/olympic-programme-commission. Retrieved: 16 May, 2022.

IOC (December 2021b). Factsheet – Women in the Olympic Movement. https://stillmed.olympics.com/media/Documents/Olympic-Movement/Factsheets/Women-in-the-Olympic-Movement.pdf

IPC (24 August, 2021a). Tokyo 2020 sets the record for most athletes and women at a Paralympic Games. https://www.paralympic.org/news/tokyo-2020-sets-record-most-athletes-and-women-paralympic-games. Retrieved: 1 September, 2021.

IPC (November, 2021b). *Beijing 2022 Paralympic Winter Games – Qualification Regulations.* https://www.paralympic.org/sites/default/files/2021-11/2021_11_23_QC_Beijing2022_v1.8.pdf.

IPC (4 March 2022). Record number of female Para athletes set for Beijing 2022 Paralympic Winter Games. https://www.paralympic.org/feature/record-number-female-para-athletes-set-beijing-2022-paralympic-winter-games. Retrieved: 6 March, 2022.

ISSF (20 February 2017). ISSF Press Release—ISSF Executive Committee and Administrative Council meet to discuss Tokyo 2020 Olympic Program recommendations. https://www.issf-sports.org/getfile.aspx?mod=docf&pane=1&inst=340&iist=82&file=20170220%20ISSF%20Press%20Release%2002.pdf. Retrieved: 13 January, 2021.

Leigh, Mary H. & Thérèse M. Bonin (1977). The pioneering role of Madam Alice Milliat and FSFI in establishing international track and field competition for women. *Journal of Sport History*, 4(1), 72–83.

Lenskyj, Helen (1990). Power and play: Gender and sexuality issues in sport and physical activity. *International Review for the Sociology of Sport*, 23(3), 235–245.

McLachlan, Fiona (2016). Gender politics, the Olympic Games, and Road Cycling: The case for critical history. *The International Journal of the History of Sport*, 33(4), 469–483.

Official Programme of the Olympic Games Paris 2024 (7 December, 2020).

Olympic Games Tripartite Commission Invitation Places – Allocation Procedures and Regulations (Games of the XXXI Olympiad, Rio 2016) (10 April 2014).

Pape, Madeleine (2020). Gender segregation and trajectories of organizational change: The underrepresentation of women in sport leadership. *Gender & Society*, 34(1), 81–105.

Paralympic Games Left Behind in the Race towards Gender Equality, UBC Expert Says (3 March 2022). https://news.ubc.ca/2022/03/03/paralympic-games-left-behind-in-the-race-towards-gender-equality-ubc-expert-says/. Retrieved: 1 May, 2022.

Qualification System – Games of the XXXI Olympiad – Rio 2016: Fédération Internationale de Natation – Swimming (March 2015).

Qualification System – Games of the XXXI Olympiad – Rio 2016: International Canoe Federation – Canoe Sprint (July 2014).

Qualification System – Games of the XXXII Olympiad – Tokyo 2020: International Canoe Federation – Canoe Sprint (December 2019).

Rowbottom, Mike (14 November 2021). New ICF President Konietzko looking for evolution rather than revolution after Olympic changes. https://www.insidethegames.biz/articles/1115448/icf-president-konietzko-perurena-ioc-sup. Retrieved: 20 November, 2021.

Summer Paralympic Games Overview (n.d.). https://www.paralympic.org/paralympic-games/summer-overview. Retrieved: 20 February, 2021.

Tuggle, Charles A. & Anne Owen (1999). A descriptive analysis of NBC's coverage of the centennial Olympics: The "Games of the Woman"? *Journal of Sport and Social* Issues, 23(2), 171–182.

UN Women (n.d.). Gender equality glossary. https://trainingcentre.unwomen.org/mod/glossary/view.php?id=36.

UNESCO (June, July, August 2015). *Gender Wire – Division for Gender Equality.* N° 1.

Walton, Theresa A. (2003). Title IX: Forced to wrestle up the backside. *Women's Sport and Physical Activity Journal*, 12(2), 5–26.

Winter Paralympic Games Overview (n.d.). https://www.paralympic.org/paralympic-games/winter-overview. Retrieved: 20 February, 2021.

World Sailing (9 June 2017). World Sailing respond to the IOC sports programme announcement for Tokyo 2020. https://tokyo2020.sailing.org/2017/06/09/world-sailing-respond-to-the-ioc-sports-programme-announcement-for-tokyo-2020/. Retrieved: 19 June, 2019.

3

A QUALITATIVE ANALYSIS OF GENDER INEQUALITIES AND THE OLYMPIC PROGRAMME

Beyond the numbers

Introduction

In *Agenda 2020*, the "strategic roadmap" for the Olympic Movement, the IOC (2014) includes Recommendation 11: "Foster gender equality". The primary strategy offered to "foster gender equality" is: "The IOC to work with the International Federations to achieve 50 per cent female participation in the Olympic Games and to stimulate women's participation and involvement in sport by creating more participation opportunities at the Olympic Games" (IOC, 2014). The IOC has consistently promoted a version of gender equality that would be more accurately called gender parity. As introduced previously, "Gender parity: it's about numbers! The goal is to reach a balanced ration of women and men (ideally, 50/50) in terms of representation and participation at all levels" (Gender Wire, UNESCO, 2015). Parity is a quantitative objective and, while it is part of gender equality, achieving gender parity cannot be understood as achieving gender equality in the sense of equal status. Specifically, "Women and men can fully realize their fundamental rights and have equal opportunities and rights to access and contribute [...], and to benefit from the results" (Gender Wire, UNESCO, 2015). In order to offer a more complete story about gender equality at the Olympic Games, it is necessary to explore the conditions of women's participation relative to men, and the ways that women athletes and women's events are included on the Olympic programme relative to men athletes and men's events.

As discussed in the Introduction, both the IOC and some IFs fiercely resisted women's inclusion at the Olympic Games. It was only when the IOC perceived threats to its monopoly over elite, amateur, international sport that it encouraged IFs to take over governance of the women's versions of their sports, and began to include more women's events on the Olympic programme. The early

DOI: 10.4324/9781003002741-3

emphasis on limiting women's participation both in terms of numbers (to not "cast a shadow over the men") and in terms of sports and events (only those "suited to their sex") continues to influence the composition of the Olympic programme today.

In this chapter, I explore gender equality in a way the IOC has not addressed – in terms of the gendered experiences of sport that are the result of institutionalized differences (developed by the IFs) in the sports and disciplines in which both men and women compete at the Olympic Games.[1] First, I introduce the concept of sport typing, which I argue can be applied to entire sports, but also to *within* sport differences. After a brief discussion about gender-exclusive sports and disciplines included on the Olympic sport programme, I detail the categories of gendered differences between men's and women's conditions of participation in the same sport. These include differences in the length of races, available weight categories, the height, weight, size, and spacing of equipment and the size of venue, and a final category that includes differences in judging, rules, and uniforms.

Sport typing

Metheny (1965) developed the concept of sport typing through an attempt to identify sports that are considered appropriate for men and sports that are considered appropriate for women based on the cultural expectations of gender in a specific culture. Sport typing suggests that some sports are *typed* as feminine, and other sports are *typed* as masculine. Using a study of attitudes of college women in the United States, and the Olympic sport programme for women athletes at the time, Metheny (1965: 51) determined that

1 It is *not appropriate* for women to engage in contests in which:
   the resistance of the *opponent* is overcome by bodily contact
   the resistance of a *heavy object* is overcome by direct application of bodily force
   the body is projected into or through space over long distances or for extended periods of time

According to Metheny (1965: 49), this included Olympic competitions in "Wrestling, judo, boxing, weight-lifting, hammer throw, pole vault, the longer foot races, high hurdles, and all forms of team games – with the recent exception of volleyball". Metheny (1965: 51) also identified contests in which "It *may be appropriate* for women identified in the lower levels of socioeconomic status" to engage, as well as contests in which "It is *wholly appropriate*" for all women to engage based on how their bodies are expected to move in relation to opponents and/or equipment. Although Metheny (1965: 52, 53) offers a biologically essentialist explanation for some of the existing differences between men's and women's appropriate sport participation, she acknowledges that "The facets of biology provide no logical basis of support for these relative distinctions" – distinctions such as women being able to then participate in the shot put, discus, and javelin, but not the hammer throw at the Olympic Games. Metheny (1965: 48) emphasized that "the socially sanctioned images of femininity and masculinity are always relative" and grounded her typology of gender-appropriate sports in the concept of cultural expectations about gender. From the outset, Metheny allows for, and in fact, requires, that the typology be updated to reflect changing beliefs about femininity and masculinity.

In fact, Metheny (1965: 171) claims, "Within our own 'women's sports' and women's patterns of competition, both the range of sports and the intensity of competition have greatly increased during the past 20 years". Kane (1995: 193) challenged the continued use of the concept of sport typing, calling for an understanding of a sport continuum:

> In spite of all the efforts to the contrary, there exists today a sport *continuum* in which many women routinely outperform many men and, in some cases, women outperform most—if not all—men in a variety of sports and physical skills/activities. The acknowledgement of such a continuum could provide a direct assault on traditional beliefs about sport—and gender itself—as an inherent, oppositional binary grounded in biological difference.

However, Kane's (1995: 193) belief that this awareness "could serve as an important vehicle for resistance and transformation" has not been realized in the realm of Olympic sport, and particularly, at the Olympic Games. The "efforts to the contrary" continue to have a significant influence on the ways that sport is organized – and organized differently for men and women – and represented. Theberge (1998: 196) explains the sport continuum as "an argument for considering ways in which ideological and material conditions reproduce the view that sport is a naturally occurring binary divided along gender lines" (Theberge, 1998: 196). It is those ideological and material conditions that continue to inform an understanding of sport (both entire sports and differentiated modes of participating in sports) as appropriate for men or appropriate for women.

According to Kane (1995: 196) acknowledging a sport continuum addresses a major limitation of previous approaches to understanding resistance and transformation through sport: "the unintended implication that there are two kinds of sport (women's and men's) and that women cannot compete adequately with men in those sports that 'matter most—those traditionally associated with men". Kane (1995: 196) raises the case of "women's achievements in sports traditionally identified as male", and Theberge (1998) extends this to her research about women's ice hockey. Theberge (1998: 184) claims, "A focus on women in team-oriented confrontational sports is a particularly powerful challenge to the construction of sport as an oppositional binary that 'naturally' reproduces gender divisions". However, IFs continue to make decisions about the organization of sport that differentiates men's and women's participation, such that direct comparisons are not possible. For example, "The rules of women's and men's hockey are substantially the same, with the exception that the rules of women's hockey prohibit intentional body checking, that is, intentional efforts to hit or take out an opponent" (Theberge, 1998: 185). This one exception in the rules of ice hockey results in significant differences in the ways that men hockey players and women hockey players experience the sport, and perhaps just as importantly, in the messages sent to the audience about men's and women's relative suitability for full contact play. In this chapter, I will argue that in sports on the Olympic programme, we continue to see evidence of the construction of sport in ways that reproduce ideas about natural differences between men and women. Further, sports and disciplines are constructed in ways that reinforce notions about men athletes' superiority over women athletes, with respect to the skills required such as endurance and strength.

There are two main points that inform the remainder of this chapter. First, sport on the Olympic programme is often organized in ways that preclude acknowledgement of a sport continuum. In some cases, this is because of gender-exclusive disciplines that are reminiscent of Metheny's sport types, such as only men wrestlers competing in Greco Roman Wrestling and only women gymnasts competing in Rhythmic Gymnastics. I will also make the case for another "type" of sport typing – where Metheny's approach refers to *between* sport typing, I will demonstrate the prevalent use of *within* sport typing among sports at the Olympic Games. This refers to the ways that IFs institutionalize gender-differentiated forms of participation for men and women in the same sports. This differentiation is accomplished through differences in the structure of events (e.g., length of races, number of weight categories) and in the rules of participation (e.g., the rules of play, as well as age restrictions, uniforms). These decisions about the organization of sport ensure that

> we are never allowed to see women outperform men in the real sports [those traditionally associated with men] or are never [or very rarely] allowed to witness women possessing physical attributes and skills that have been traditionally associated with men.
>
> *(Kane, 1995: 203)*

This is only possible in the larger context of sport organized on the principle of sex segregation. Channon et al. (2016: 1112) argue,

> the continuation of sex segregation has left something of a discursive 'back door' through which ideals of male athletic superiority can escape unscathed, retaining their influence over wider cultural belief systems. While allowing for the admission that women can be strong, competitive, resilient, etc., the culture of segregated sport continues to insist that they will never be able to be these things in ways which compare favourably to men.

Even in sports where men and women athletes are celebrated for possessing traditionally masculine physical attributes and skills, such as Weightlifting, their participation is sufficiently differentiated – through the organization and number of weight categories, and use of different equipment – that their performances cannot be directly compared. And, as detailed below, when sports and events are gender-differentiated, women's participation is consistently organized as *less than* the men's version. In the case of Weightlifting, there are fewer weight categories for women (at Rio 2016, there were eight weight categories for men and seven for women). Women lifters have a much smaller range between the lowest and highest weight categories (27kg for women and 49kg for men), further limiting women's participation. And, the bars women use are different from the men's in at least seven ways, including the weight, length, and distance between grip sections on the bar.

The second main point is that not all sports on the Olympic programme are organized in ways that emphasize gender-differentiated participation (though *all* are organized as sex-segregated, with the exception of mixed-gender events). It is these internal contradictions – especially between sports that are similar – on the sport programme, as much as an assessment of the IOC's commitment to gender equality, that demands scrutiny of the sports and events at the Olympic Games. World Triathlon determines that men and women triathletes compete over the same distances in each of the swimming (1,500m), cycling (43km), and running (10km) components of the Triathlon. However, in Road Cycling at Rio 2016, the Union Cycliste Internationale (UCI) had men cyclists ride 241.5km in the road race (the event most similar to the cycling portion of the Triathlon), and women cyclists rode 141km. In the time trial, men cyclists rode 54.2km and women cyclists rode only 29.8km. Women's and men's participation in both Badminton and Table Tennis is nearly identical, with some differences in the uniforms the athletes are allowed – but not required – to wear. But in Tennis, from Atlanta 1996 until Rio 2016, the men's singles final was determined in five sets, while all other Tennis finals were determined in three sets. The International Tennis Federation (ITF) made the change to a men's singles three-set final for Tokyo 2020 citing "concerns of overplay for players who reach the latter stages" in multiple Tennis events (one tennis player could compete in singles, doubles, and mixed doubles competition at the Games) (SportBusiness Staff, 2019). In Field Hockey at the Summer Games, men's and women's teams compete using the same rules, equipment, and tournament organization. In Ice Hockey at the Winter Games, men's and women's teams compete using different rules about body checking (prohibited for women), different requirements about safety equipment (men are required to wear a half face shield and women are required to wear a full face shield), as well as a different number of athletes on each team (25 men and 23 women) and teams in the tournament (12 and 10 at Beijing 2022). (These numbers are discussed further in chapter 2.)

The Fédération Internationale de Volleyball (FIVB) dictates that the net height for women's Beach Volleyball and indoor Volleyball is 2.24m, while in the men's events, the net height is 2.34m. In Basketball, which also uses a type of net (or hoop) as an integral part of the game, the International Basketball Federation (FIBA) does not distinguish between its height for men and women, but it does require that the ball women play with is smaller in circumference and lighter in weight than the ball the men play with. Each of these examples demonstrates that some IFs organize their sports and events in ways that can be considered gender equal, while many others continue to use *within* sport typing as a strategy to differentiate men's and women's participation. Further, these examples reveal that the explanations that many perceive to be "common sense", such as justifying different net heights in Volleyball because men, on average, are taller than women, on average, are not consistent across Olympic sports. This undermines the – already limited – explanatory power of appeals to differences in men's and women's biology. How, then, were these decisions made in the first place, and how do they remain – in so many sports – unquestioned aspects of the organization of that sport? Focusing attention on gender equality *beyond* the numbers, to include the differences in men's and women's conditions of participation, is necessary not only to answer these questions but also to work towards a more substantive achievement of gender equality.

Gender exclusive sports and disciplines[2]

Kane and Snyder (1989) emphasize the importance of physicality in the original conception of (between) sport typing. They argued, "'Gender-appropriateness' is determined by how much a particular sport requires a female to be gender-consistent or gender-challenging to traditional definitions of femininity", and gender-consistency is determined by what the woman athlete is expected to do with her body (Kane & Snyder, 1989: 81). At the "appropriately feminine" extreme of this binary conception are sports in which a woman athlete "uses her body in aesthetically pleasing ways (gymnastics), or uses light instruments to overcome light objects (tennis, golf)" (Kane & Snyder, 1989: 81). At the "appropriately masculine" extreme are sports in which a woman athlete "uses her body as an instrument of physical power—by subduing an opponent through the use of physical force (football, rugby)" (Kane & Snyder, 1989: 81). These seemingly outdated, stereotypical categories of sport are really quite accurate representations of some of the gender exclusive disciplines that remain on the Olympic sport programme. At the Summer Games, Rhythmic Gymnastics and Artistic Swimming are contested only by women athletes. These disciplines each highlight – through their organization as subjectively judged and the specific criteria included by the FIG (Fédération Internationale Gymnastique) and Fédération Internationale de Natation (FINA) in their scoring systems – artistry or artistic impression (including the athletes' appearance and ability to use the musical accompaniment to tell a story), alongside difficulty and execution. The only remaining entire discipline that is contested only by men at the Summer Games is Greco Roman Wrestling. According to United World Wrestling (UWW), the primary difference between the Freestyle Wrestling discipline (in which both men and women compete) and Greco Roman Wrestling is that in the former, "all holds can involve the legs in order to ultimately pin the opponent's shoulders to the mat", while in the latter "The holds can only be executed by means of the upper body" (UWW, 2022). The idea that Greco Roman Wrestling somehow involves greater use of "physical force" is unsupported by this difference, which means that the men-only discipline clearly fits the masculine sport type, but so does the discipline in which women do compete. This is another example of internal contradictions – this time, within the same sport – with respect to sport typing on the Olympic programme.

Other examples of gender-exclusive sports at the Summer and Winter Games are even more challenging to explain using the concepts of between sport typing and gender appropriateness. Until Tokyo 2020, the International Canoe Federation (ICF) organized Kayak slalom and sprint events for both men and women paddlers, and excluded women paddlers from any Canoe events (also slalom and sprint disciplines) during the entire time the sport has been at the Olympic Games. According to the ICF (n.d.), the difference between Canoe and Kayak

> is relatively simple; it's related to the athlete's position in the boat and the type of paddle they use to propel the boat. In a kayak, the paddler is seated and uses a double-bladed paddle [...]. In a canoe, the paddler kneels and uses a single-bladed paddle [...].

There is nothing about this description that suggests one sport would be considered now – or at some time in the past – more appropriately feminine. Further, the ICF includes women paddlers in Canoe events at ICF World Championships and other international-level competitions. Beginning with the limited inclusion of women's Ski Jumping at Sochi 2014, women compete in all but one sport at the Winter Olympic Games. The FIS has organized Nordic Combined events – in which skiers compete in both cross-country skiing and ski jumping – exclusively for men since the first Winter Olympic Games in Chamonix in 1924. There currently seems to be little justification for the continued exclusion of women skiers from Nordic Combined; certainly not in terms of assumed gender-based biological or physical differences. I do recognize that there are other factors influencing IF and IOC decisions about which women's sports and disciplines to include (and exclude) from the Olympic sport programme. These include the popularity of, and level of competition in, the sport or discipline for women internationally. As McLachlan (2016: 479) reminds us, we cannot simply celebrate women's inclusion at the Games: "While women's events are 'included' it cannot be concluded that this is evidence of progress in terms of equality between the sexes". Ultimately, when there are not equal (or even equivalent) opportunities for men and women athletes to compete at the Olympic Games, these need to be addressed in the conversations – and recommendations – about achieving gender equality at the Games.

Within sport typing

Given the small number of gender-exclusive sports and disciplines remaining at the Olympic Games, the vast majority of the programme is composed of events in which both men and women athletes compete. This may sound like a possible gender equality achievement for the IOC; however, as explored in the previous chapter in terms of numbers, and in this chapter in terms of the conditions of participation, such a broad statement requires close attention and analysis. According to the *Olympic Charter*, one element of the mission and role of the IOC (2021) is "to encourage and support the promotion of women in sport at all levels and in all structures with a view to implementing the principle of equality of men and women". From any understanding of gender equality, the myriad differences between men's and women's participation at the Olympic Games do not constitute gender equality. Aspects of within-sport typing – differentiating between the ways that men and women compete in the same (or equivalent) events – are pervasive on the Olympic sport programme. Donnelly (forthcoming) found that almost 65% of the 306 events at Rio 2016 included formalized gender-based differences in men and women athletes' participation. In this section, I explain and offer examples of a number of categories of difference that appear on the Olympic programme. These categories build on those developed by Donnelly and Donnelly (2013), which provide a model for "auditing" gender equality at the Olympic (and other multi-sport) Games. Men's and women's participation in the same events – beyond the numbers – may be differentiated with respect to (1) length of races; (2) available weight categories (in sports organized by weight classes) and weight limits; (3) height, weight, size, and spacing of equipment used and/or size of the venue; and (4) rules and uniforms.

At the Olympic Games, fans in the stands and viewers at home *see* what sports are included, which events within those sports, as well as how athletes play those sports, what they wear to play, and the equipment they use. These most accessible, observable elements of the Olympic sport programme are not natural, nor are they neutral. Rather, they are the result of the beliefs and values, including those about gender, of those in charge of the Olympic Games (primarily the IOC and IFs). The IOC's commitment to gender equality must also be assessed in these terms. IFs that choose to differentiate between men's and women's events using one of the four categories of difference identified typically use more than one of those categories. McLachlan (2016: 478) explains the connection between decisions to implement gender-based differentiation and gender inequality:

> The issue with classification or categorization is not in and of itself problematic. What is problematic and which has been identified in the research is the judgement placed on that categorization, or when individuals are seen not to fit the expectations associated to that category.

In each category of difference, it is apparent that *when* sports and events are gender-differentiated (acknowledging that some are not), women's participation is organized as *less than* the men's version. The men's event is frequently used as the "norm", and the women's event is designed as a deviation from that norm, often in ways that may be interpreted as minimizing. To be clear, I am not suggesting that women athletes' capabilities, skills, and successes are in any way diminished or minimized by the ways their events are organized (something over which both men and women athletes have had little or no control). There are many examples including and beyond Olympic sports, in which the rules (and/or equipment, venue, scoring, and so on) have been changed when girls and women begin to play a sport in which boys' and men's competition is already established; often referred to as playing by the "girls' rules".

In each of the following sections, I include examples of events on the Summer and Winter Olympic Games' sport programmes. These examples are not exhaustive but have been selected as most illustrative of each category of gender differentiation.

Length of races

Women and men compete over the same distances in some of the longest races at the Summer Olympic Games. Both men and women run 42km in the marathon in Athletics and swim 10km in the open water Swimming marathon event. As discussed, both men and women triathletes swim (1,500m), cycle (43km), and run (10km). Despite this, there continue to be – sometimes significant – differences in the length of men's and women's races in other sports at both the Summer and Winter Olympic Games. In Athletics, men and women compete over the same distances in most races; however, while World Athletics has included a 20km racewalk event for both men and women at the Games, only men have competed in the 50km racewalk event (which will be replaced by a mixed gender racewalk event at Paris 2024). In Swimming, FINA equalized the race distances in all men's and women's events at Tokyo 2020 by adding an 800m freestyle event for men (previously only for women) and a 1,500m freestyle event for women (previously only for men). The UCI organizes some of the most unequal race distances for men and women in the Cycling disciplines. In Mountain Biking, men and women ride the same course; however, men mountain bikers complete seven laps of the course, while women complete six (each lap is between 4 and 6km long). The most glaring differences between men's and women's race distances are found in Road Cycling. At both Rio 2016 and Tokyo 2020, the UCI organized a women's road race course that was almost 100km shorter than the men's, and women cyclists rode only one lap of the time trial course, while the men cyclists rode two laps (a 29.8km course at Rio 2016 and a 22.1km course at Tokyo 2020). In every case where there is a difference in the race distance for men and women athletes, women always compete over a shorter distance than men.

The same is true in almost all of the races included on the programme at the Winter Olympic Games. In Speed Skating at Pyeongchang 2018, men and women competed in many races held over equal distances. The exceptions were the relay event in Short Track – 5,000m for men and 3,000m for women – and the longest distances in Long Track Speed Skating – 10,000m for men and 5,000m for women. The Fédération Internationale de Ski (FIS) governs all of the Skiing and Snowboarding disciplines, and most races are different lengths for men and women. In Alpine Skiing at Pyeongchang 2018, men's races consistently started at a higher point on the hill than women's races. For example, the downhill course was 2,852m long for men and 2,499m long for women, and the super giant slalom course was 2,217m long for men and 1,982m long for women. In Cross Country Skiing men ski a longer distance than women in every style of race (Table 3.1).

In May 2022, 57% of members of the FIS Cross Country Committee voted to equalize men's and women's race distances for the 2022–2023 World Cup season (FIS, 2022). Of note, the committee appears to have standardized most of the distances at a length between the existing men's and women's distances: 10, 20, and 50km. It is important that IFs not simply reinforce the notion of the men's events as the "norm" when making decisions about race distances. Run Equal, an organization whose "current focus is on campaigning to equalise the distance run by women and men in cross-country events" emphasizes, "Equalising race distances doesn't mean change what the women run to be the same as men'. It never has. Assuming the men's race is the untouchable standard' reflects perfectly the bigger problem we have here" (RunEqual (@run_equal) 20 January, 2021 tweet).

According to the FIS (2022) press release about the decision to equalize the World Cup race distances,

> The National Ski Federations, of which the voting members consist, did not go into a long discussion but came with a clear opinion. All up front, the main argument to vote for equal distances was that there should not be any question whether women were capable of racing the same distances as men, as they prove that they physically are capable of doing so already. The main argument against was the time that women need to cover the same distance as men and the effective TV time.

The relationship between decisions about race distance and scheduling (especially for television events) seems to be a consideration in other sports as well. For

TABLE 3.1 Cross Country Skiing race distances for men and women

Event	*Men's distance*	*Women's distance*
Classical	15km	10km
Mass start	50km	30km
Skiathlon	30km	15km
Relay	4 × 10km	4 × 5km

example, for Mountain Biking, the UCI has set a preferred amount of time in which the race should take place; a minimum of 90 minutes and a maximum of 105 minutes. The argument, then, is that the relative difference between men's and women's finishing times (on average, slower for women) warrants women's participation in a shorter distance race. IFs need to make decisions about race distances that, first, make the most sense for the athletes competing in those races. The various other considerations that influence their decision-making need to be secondary, and they also need to be shared publicly.

Like Cross Country Skiing, Biathlon is organized into different styles of races in which men always ski longer distances than women (Table 3.2). In every event, biathletes alternate between cross-country skiing and shooting a rifle, with at least two bouts of shooting in each race (five targets each time, from standing and prone positions). Biathletes are penalized for each target they miss when in the shooting range. In the individual event, biathletes incur a one-minute penalty for each missed target, that is, if an athlete misses two targets, two minutes are added to their overall time. In the other Biathlon events, biathletes must ski a penalty loop for each missed target; one 150m lap for each miss. The penalties for missing targets are the same for men and women biathletes, which means that women biathletes seem to be punished more severely than the men. That is, there is no equivalent reduction in the penalty loop distance relative to the race distance. If there is a justifiable reason to differentiate the race distances for men and women biathletes, it seems that the same justification should be applied to the application of penalties. One of the biggest challenges when studying the Olympic sport programme is inferring the priorities and intentions of IFs (and the IOC) based on the decisions they have made "behind closed doors". As part of the IOC's recommendation to "foster gender equality", IFs should be required to review their existing event offerings and explain each instance of *within* sport typing.

Available weight categories and weight limits

In the previous chapter, I detailed the greater number of weight categories in some sports organized by weight classes on the Olympic programme. In Boxing, Weightlifting, and Wrestling, there have typically been not only more weight

TABLE 3.2 Biathlon race distances for men and women

Event	*Men's distance*	*Women's distance*
Individual	20km	15km
Mass start	15km	12.5km
Pursuit	12.5km	10km
Sprint	10km	7.5km
Relay	4 × 7.5km	4 × 6km

TABLE 3.3 Weight range for men and women in sports divided by weight classes

	Lowest men's weight class	*Highest men's weight class*	***Range for men***	*Lowest women's weight class*	*Highest women's weight class*	***Range for women***
Boxing (10M, 3W)	49kg	+91kg	**+42kg**	51kg	+75kg	**+24kg**
Judo	−60kg	+100kg	**+40kg**	−48kg	+78kg	**+30kg**
Taekwondo	−58kg	+80kg	**+22kg**	−49kg	+67kg	**+18kg**
Weightlifting (8M, 7W)	56kg	+108kg	**+49kg**	48kg	+75kg	**+27kg**
Wrestling (freestyle)	57kg	125kg	**+68kg**	48kg	75kg	**+27kg**

categories for men but also more men in each weight category (due to higher athlete quota numbers). This is directly contradicted by Judo and Taekwondo that have had an equal number of weight categories for men and women since at least London 2012. In this section, I focus on the ways that organizing different weight categories for men and women influences who can participate and how they participate. In particular, across the sports organized into weight classes, there is always a narrower range of weight classes for women. Specifically, the difference between the lowest weight class and the highest weight class is always greater for men athletes than for women athletes. At Rio 2016, there was appreciably more diversity in the range of weight classes available to men than to women (Table 3.3). Overall, this means men have not only numerically more opportunities to participate but also that men with a wider range of body weights are able to participate at the Olympic Games.

In a small number of sports, IFs set a weight limit for athletes and/or a combined weight limit for the athlete and the equipment they use. World Rowing includes two weight-limited events at the Olympic Games. In the single sculls event, the maximum weight for men is 72.5kg and the maximum weight for women in 59kg. In the men's lightweight double sculls event, each rower must weigh a minimum of 55kg and a maximum of 72.5kg; the average weight of both rowers must be 70kg. In the women's lightweight double sculls event, each rower must weigh a minimum of 50kg and a maximum of 59kg; the average weight of both rowers must be 57kg. Consistent with the sports that are divided into weight classes, men rowers in the lightweight double sculls event have a larger range of acceptable weight than the women rowers – 17.5kg for men and only 9kg for women – which means there are opportunities for men with a greater diversity of bodyweights than for women. At the Winter Olympic Games, all Bobsleigh, Skeleton (governed by the International Bobsleigh and Skeleton Federation (IBSF)), and Luge (governed by the Fédération Internationale de Luge (FIL)) events have maximum weights for the participating athletes and for the combined weight of the athlete and sled. Each sport uses a different kind of sled. In Bobsleigh, women and men both compete in a two-man event (women also competed in a monobob event for the first time at Beijing 2022 and men also compete in a four-man event). The minimum weight of the men's and women's sleds is 170kg, and the maximum weight – including the crew and other racing equipment – is 390kg for men and 330kg for women. In Skeleton, the maximum weight of the men's sled is 45kg and the maximum weight of the women's sled is 38kg. The combined weight of the athlete and race equipment (including the sled) is 120kg for men and 102kg for women. This makes the maximum weight for Skeleton athletes 75kg for men and 54kg for women.

In singles Luge, the FIL has set a total weight limit – of the athlete plus race clothing (4kg) plus the sled (23kg), and additional weight (up to 13kg for men and 10kg for women) – of 117kg for men and 102kg for women. Based on the FIL's calculation, this means the maximum body weight for men lugers is 90kg and for women lugers is 75kg. In every case of a weight limit for athletes at the Olympic Games, men's weights are heavier than women's. When the heavier weight of the athlete and sled is understood as an advantage on the sliding track, limits to that weight make sense. It is not clear, however, how the IBSF and FIL have determined the relative weight limits for men's and women's events, and if these weight limits are able to accommodate the athletes who are interested in participating in these sports. It seems that the most inclusive option – for men and women – may be to divide the competition into weight classes. This would allow more men and more women to compete in each of Rowing, Bobsleigh, Skeleton, and Luge, rather than limiting the pool of participants based on body weight. However, as demonstrated by the current sports on the Olympic programme that are divided into weight classes, there needs to be attention to both: (1) Equalizing the number of weight classes available for men and women; and (2) Assessing the weight classes to determine their relevance for the athletes participating.

Height, weight, size, and spacing of equipment used and/or size of the venue

Men's and women's participation is differentiated in a variety of ways with respect to the equipment athletes use and the venues in which they play. In fact, the number of types of differences is quite overwhelming. In this section, I offer examples of events in which men and women athletes use different equipment, sports in which the ball that men's and women's teams play with is differentiated, and events in which there are differences between the playing venue for men and women athletes.

Despite men's and women's participation in almost all of the same events in *Athletics*, there is ample evidence of *within* sport typing in the hurdles and the field events. Men and women sprinters compete in two races with hurdles on the track: 110m for men; 100m for women; and 400m for men and women. World

TABLE 3.4 Measurement specifications for men's and women's javelins

	Men's javelin	*Women's javelin*
Weight	800g	600g
Length	2.6–2.7m	2.2–2.3m
Distance from tip of metal head to centre of gravity	900–1,060mm	800–920mm
Distance from tail to centre of gravity	1,540–1,800mm	1280–1,500mm
Width of cord grip	150–160mm	140–150mm
Diameter of shaft at thickest point	25–30mm	20–25mm

Athletics dictates that the 10 hurdles for the men's 110m race are 1.067m high and spaced 9.14m apart and for the women's 100m race, the 10 hurdles are 0.838m high and spaced 8.5m apart. In the 400m race, men's hurdles are 0.914m high and women's hurdles are 0.762m high (for both, 10 hurdles are placed 35m apart). The field events include discus, hammer, javelin, and shot put. In each case, women athletes use equipment – the discus, hammer, javelin, and shot – that is smaller, lighter, and shorter than the equipment men athletes use. For example, World Athletics determines that the men's shot weighs 7.2kg and measures 110–130mm in diameter, while the women's shot weighs 4kg and measures 95–110mm in diameter. The javelin is differentiated on every dimension (Table 3.4).

As mentioned, there are also many differences in the requirements for the bars that men weightlifters and women weightlifters use, including the weight, total length, length of the outer ends, length of each grip section, the distance between the two grip sections, and the size of the rim diameter. No matter the rationale for these differences, it is notable that people (most often men in decision-making positions in IFs) have made these decisions to differentiate – in such specific, almost minute, terms – the ways in which men and women participate in their sports. In each case, this means that men's and women's performances cannot be directly compared. Even if a man and woman were to lift the same amount of weight in Olympic competition, or run a similar time in a hurdles race, the differences in weight categories and equipment ensure that their results are not comparable.

Shooting offers a particularly interesting example of differences between the equipment used by men and women athletes, in this case, pistols, rifles, and shotguns. Historically, Shooting was a nominally open competition at the Games; women could compete in men's pistol and rifle events from 1968 to 1980, and in skeet and trap events until 1992, though very few women did. Shooting has been entirely separated into men's and women's events since Atlanta 1996, with women's events in skeet and trap introduced at Sydney 2000. Teetzel (2009) posits that the motivation for this was Zhang Shan's (a woman shooter) gold medal win in the skeet event at Barcelona 1992. In the era of open competition, there were presumably regulations about the shooters' equipment; however, it is highly unlikely that there were gendered regulations, e.g., that men's and women's rifles should weigh different amounts. These equipment-based distinctions were introduced with sex-segregated competition, alongside differences in the events themselves (e.g., the number of shots, time for each shot). For example, at London 2012, the International Shooting Sports Federation (ISSF) dictated that women's pistols could weigh no more than 1,400g, have a 153mm maximum barrel length, and a 220m maximum sight radius length. No equivalent restrictions on men's pistols were listed. In rifle events, men shooters used a rifle that weighed 8kg, while women shooters' rifle weighed 6.5kg. Decisions made to differentiate men's and women's competitions were likely used for two main purposes: (1) They served as a justification of the need for sex-segregated Shooting events; and (2) They ensured that men's and women's results could not be directly compared. These examples of *within* sport typing, introduced the idea that women shooters need different competition conditions than their men counterparts. This, in spite of the fact that men and women had previously competed against each other in open competition. In the 2017 ISSF *Official Statutes Rules and Regulations*, the differences between men's and women's equipment had been removed, which further calls into question whether they were ever a necessary part of Shooting competition.

The fact that some ball sports differentiate between the ball used by men and the ball used by women, while others do not, is another case in which the justification for these differences is seemingly suspect. Specifically, in Field Hockey, Football, Golf, Rugby, Table Tennis, Tennis, Beach Volleyball, and Volleyball, men and women play with the same-sized ball. In Basketball, Handball, and Water Polo, men and women play with a different sized ball – measured by circumference, weight, and in Water Polo, by the pressure to which the ball is inflated – and in each sport, the women's ball is smaller, lighter, and inflated to lower pressure. Both Basketball and Handball are otherwise gender-equal sports, including the same venue, rules, uniform requirements, as well as the number of athletes on a team and teams in the tournament for men and women. The ball is not the only gender-based difference in Water Polo; the length of the pool may also be differentiated (and there were 12 men's teams and eight women's teams in the tournaments at Rio 2016). For both men's and women's Water Polo games, the minimum distance between the goal lines is 20m, but for men, the maximum distance is 30m, and for women, the maximum distance is 25m. It is unclear how FINA would justify this 5m difference when men and women compete over the same distances in all other Swimming events in the pool.

While the FIVB does not differentiate the ball used by men's and women's teams in Beach Volleyball and Volleyball, they do enforce that the net is set higher for men's games (2.43m) than for women's games (2.24m). In Golf, the distance to the tee at every hole is longer for men than it is for women. At Rio 2016, the average distance to the tee for men golfers was 396 yards, and for women golfers, it was 347 yards. Also, at Rio 2016, the men's and women's freestyle BMX track layouts were different. According to the UCI, the men BMX riders took the "right track in [the] second stretch of the course, [rode] two doubles, a step-down, and a huge final double leading into the second corner", and the women BMX riders took the "left track in [the] second stretch of the course, [and rode a] smaller series of doubles leading into the second corner". The description of "a smaller series of doubles" in the women's track layout, and fewer features overall, reinforces the men's event (and track layout) as the standard, and the women's event as a lesser version of that standard. In Artistic Gymnastics, men compete on six different apparatus: floor exercise, high bar, parallel bars, pommel horse, rings, and vault. Women compete on four apparatus: balance beam, floor exercise, uneven parallel bars, and vault. Not only are there more apparatuses for men, but men's and women's competition is also differentiated in terms of the judging, even on the same apparatus (floor exercise and vault). These differences are addressed in the next section.

Finally, in Athletics, men and women both compete in a combined event at the Olympic Games. The men's event, the decathlon, includes ten events contested over two days: 100m, long jump, shot put, high jump, 400m, 110m hurdles, discus, pole vault, javelin, and 1,500m (five events each day). The women's event, the heptathlon, includes seven events contested over two days: 100m hurdles, high jump, shot put, 200m, long jump, javelin, and 800m (four events on day one, three events on day two). Each of the men's races within these combined events is longer than the women's: 1,500 versus 800m and 400 versus 200m, and only men compete in the 100m, discus, and pole vault, even though women compete in the standalone version of these events at the Olympic Games (women's pole vault was added at Sydney 2000). In every case, the equipment and venues for women's events are organized as a lesser version of the men's events, requiring lighter, shorter, smaller equipment; shorter nets and distances; fewer events; and fewer and smaller features. Each of these examples of *within* sport typing reinforces stereotypical beliefs about men's athletic superiority and further reveals the limits of gender equality in many events on the Olympic programme.

Rules and uniforms

The final category of qualitative differences includes a few sub-categories. In this section, I address the language used in IF rulesets, rules that restrict athletes' ages, rules of play, organization of play, judging, and uniforms.

Gendered language

One important mode of gender differentiation that does not appear on the Olympic programme but is revealing of many IFs' approaches to the inclusion of women is the language used in rulesets. "Calling attention to this difference is important because 'Language is never neutral. An analysis of language reveals embedded social meanings, including overt and covert biases, stereotypes, and inequities' (Messner, Duncan & Jensen, 1993: 132)" (in Donnelly et al., 2015: 29). Until Beijing 2022, the two most represented IFs at the Winter Olympic Games (responsible for 60% of all events) – the FIS and International Skating Union (ISU) – both used the designation "ladies" to refer to women's competition (and "dames" in French). There is no equivalent difference in the naming of the men's events, i.e., like all IFs, the FIS and ISU use the designation "men's". According to Lerner (1976: 296):

> the term lady also imparts a tone of frivolity and lightness to the strivings and accomplishments of women. Linguists have commented that terms like lady scientist and lady doctor seem to minimize some of the anxiety that is associated with women who are successful and powerful in traditionally masculine competitive pursuits.

This language, which feels both antiquated and inappropriate in the context of women's sport, further differentiates men's and women's events by using mismatched names. Specifically, "gentlemen" might be a more equivalent term for men's events, when the women's events are referred to as "ladies'".

Before Beijing 2022, both the FIS and ISU changed the way they name women's events. The FIS voted in June 2019 "to change the official FIS terminology from 'Ladies' to 'Women' in all applicable places, i.e. documents, titles, web site, technical materials, official communications and using gender neutral terminology in FIS publications" (FIS, 2020). Sarah Lewis, FIS secretary general at the time, claimed, "Language shapes reality and people's perception at an unconscious level and therefore the language in our publications and rules needs to reflect that FIS and our Sport stands for full participation and activity for all genders" (in FIS, 2020). Two years later, the ISU voted to change the designation of women's events. According to the ISU (2021),

> The proposed change in terminology from 'Ladies' to 'Women' throughout the Special Regulations and Technical Rules of all ISU sports is in accord with the recommendation of the IOC Gender Equality Review Project that there be a fair and balanced portrayal (i.e. how women and men are presented and described) in all forms of communication and official documents, including rules and regulations.

That the ISU cites gender equality as an explanation for making this change is notable; however, it also reveals the selective ways that IFs have taken up the IOC's gender equality-related recommendations.

Now, all international sport federations (IFs) represented at the Summer and Winter Olympic Games use the designation "women's"; however, the use of gendered language in the various IF documents – especially rule sets – reveals continued assumptions about who athletes are and, arguably, minimize the involvement of women as athletes, and in other roles in sport (e.g., referees, judges). In many cases of Summer Olympic sports (26 disciplines), the rules are written using exclusively masculine pronouns to refer to athletes (e.g., "he", "his", "him").

Some IFs have added a statement at the beginning of the documents to indicate that all uses of masculine pronouns and language should be read as also applying to women participants. For example, there is a note in the World Athletics *Competition Rules* that reads: "All references in the Rules to the masculine gender shall also include references to the feminine and all references to the singular shall also include references to the plural" (Definitions, p. 16). A number of IFs claim that this decision is "for the sake of brevity" (e.g., Equestrian, Wrestling), which is unconvincing given the length of these documents, and the success of some IFs in using gender-neutral language without significantly lengthening their documents. Some IFs include figures or illustrations in the rules. In the case of Artistic Swimming, in which only women compete at the Olympic Games, the figures represent exclusively women athletes (wearing one-piece/leotard style swimsuits with chest covered). In its rules for Diving and Water Polo – disciplines in which both men and women compete at the Olympic Games – FINA uses exclusively men athletes (wearing brief-style swimsuits with chest exposed) in all figures. World Rugby's *Laws of the Game* include photographs of both men and women (and boys and girls) playing rugby.

The decision of some IFs to proceed with using exclusively masculine pronouns is an unsatisfactory approach when there are IFs whose rules are written using gender-neutral language (e.g., World Rugby's *Laws of the Game*). Gender-neutral language usage takes two main forms. First, some IFs forego the use of gendered pronouns by referring consistently to "the athlete" or "the competitor". Other IFs use more gender-inclusive language, by including both feminine and masculine pronouns together, e.g., "he/she", "him/her", which is inclusive only with respect to the binary gender categories included at the Games. As with the other categories of gender differences detailed in this chapter, there are inconsistencies with respect to the use of language and images by some IFs. Specifically, of the IFs responsible for more than one discipline on the Summer Olympic Games programme, some are consistent in their use of exclusively masculine pronouns. For example, the Fédération Internationale de Gymnastique (FIG) includes the following statement at the beginning of the official documents for each of Artistic Gymnastics, Rhythmic Gymnastics, and Trampoline: "Words designating the masculine gender shall also include the female gender, including the judges who can be male or female for each of the disciplines". Other IFs are not consistent in their use of language, either across disciplines or within disciplines. For example, FINA uses exclusively masculine pronouns in the official documents for Diving and Swimming. However, the official documents for Artistic Swimming use gender-neutral and gender-inclusive language (despite Artistic Swimming's historical organization as women only). This suggests that FINA has both the necessary understanding and capacity to revise the official documents for all of its disciplines.

Who is included in the official documents of the IFs is an aspect of representation for both men and women in sport; i.e., if the rules and documents produced by an athlete's IF do not include them (or include them only as an afterthought, e.g., a note that the masculine language applies to women as well), this sends important messages about who can and/or should participate in this sport. Revising the language of official documents should begin with the IOC's own *Olympic Charter*. The "Introduction to the Olympic Charter" section ends with this note:

> In the *Olympic Charter*, the masculine gender used in relation to any physical person (for example, names such as president, vice-president, chairman, member, leader, official, chef de mission, participant, competitor, athlete, judge, referee, member of a jury, attaché, candidate or personnel, or pronouns such as he, they or them) shall, unless there is a specific provision to the contrary, be understood as including the feminine gender.
>
> *(International Olympic Committee, 2021).*

In fact, the IOC's own 1994 Centennial Olympic Congress recommendations included: "Examine the language used in IOC publications to avoid usage that diminishes the stature and accomplishments of women" (in Wilson, 1996: 186). More recently, the *IOC Gender Equality Review Project* recommendations include a section about "portrayal", and the first recommendation is: "The IOC requires its administration to establish principles and guidelines for fair and balanced portrayal in all its forms of communication" (2018). Continuing to include this "shall be understood as including the feminine gender" note in the *Charter*, rather than ensuring the use of gender-inclusive language does not fulfil the IOC's own recommendations. Addressing the language and images used in their official documents is one relatively simple and potentially very impactful action that the IOC and IFs can take to move towards gender equality.

Age requirement

One of the rules that is differentiated for men and women in some sports is the age requirement for athletes. Beginning at Barcelona 1992, the Fédération Internationale de Football (FIFA) decided that men's football teams are required to be composed of players who are under 23 years old, and since Atlanta 1996, men's teams may include a maximum of three players who do not meet the age requirement. FIFA has not set an age restriction for women football players at the Olympic Games. There are a few possible reasons for this decision, though the most convincing is that this avoids direct competition between the men's Olympic tournament and the FIFA (Men's) World Cup. The Olympic tournament age restriction ensures that each nation's men's senior team, composed primarily of professional players, plays only at the World Cup. With no age restriction for the women's Olympic tournament, it is the same senior national teams that compete at both the FIFA Women's World Cup and the Olympic Games. Rather than a focus on competition with other events, the minimum age requirements in Artistic Gymnastics were initiated in response to concerns about younger athletes competing in women's competitions.[3]

According to Cervin (2015), a complex set of influences – including pressure from the IOC – led to the FIG implementing a minimum age for women gymnasts at the Olympic Games. Since the rule was introduced (14 years old before 1981), the FIG has periodically raised the minimum age for women gymnasts. Since 1997, women gymnasts must be 16 years old or turn 16 in the year of the Games. Cervin (2015: 57) claims that this decision was not "based on concerns about youth athletes and their welfare, but rather as part of this push to improve public relations. The FIG was again trying to reassert its position as a feminine sport for adult women". The minimum age for men gymnasts at the Olympic Games has also increased. In fact, while men gymnasts are eligible to compete at FIG World Championships when they are 16 years old, they must be (or turn) 18 during the year to compete at the Olympic Games (Kalinski et al., 2017). In a study of relative age effects in men's gymnastics, Kalinski et al. (2017: 87) found, "Based on the analysis of the age of the finalists of the different competitions at all [Olympic Games] held in the period from 1980 to 2016, it can be concluded that the male finalists were generally in their twenties". They conclude that men gymnasts benefit from a long-term training process to develop complex skills, and are stronger at this age. Notably, the minimum age requirements seem to be as much, if not more, about maintaining the gender-based expectations that men gymnasts are strong, powerful, and acrobatic, and that women gymnasts have these characteristics while also being petite, graceful, and 'feminine'.

Judged sports

Cervin (2020: 51) claims,

> Indeed, the FIG designed women's gymnastics to be inherently different from the men's sport so that it posed no threat to masculinity [...]. There could be no direct comparison between the performances of male and female athletes. To do this, the FIG modified existing apparatuses for women (e.g., the vaulting horse turned sideways) and added completely new ones (e.g., balance beam). The requirements of the ideal performance were also different. Where the men's discipline emphasized masculinity and strength, the women's emphasized femininity and fluidity. To encapsulate this, the women's sport required dance skills.

The FIG has maintained not only the different apparatuses used in men's and women's Artistic Gymnastics, but also the "requirements of the ideal performance". For the floor exercise, men gymnasts are not accompanied by music and must complete "A series of linked elements that demonstrate strength, flexibility and balance" in a maximum of 70 seconds, while women gymnasts are required to perform to music, and must complete "A series of linked elements that demonstrate strength, flexibility and artistic quality" in a maximum of 90 seconds. This is one of the few examples of women athletes competing for a longer time than men athletes in the same event.

Both the men's and women's singles events in Figure Skating are comprised of a short program and a long program (also called the free skate). In the short program, both men and women figure skaters skate for two minutes and 40 seconds, and skaters must complete seven required elements. Five of the seven elements (double or triple axel jump, two spins, spin combination, step sequence) are the same for men and women. The two elements that differ are both related to jumps – men figure skaters are required to complete a triple or quadruple jump and a jump combination that consists of a double jump and a triple jump *or* two triple jumps *or* a quadruple jump and a double or triple jump. Quadruple jumps are not included, even as an option, in the required elements for women's singles figure skaters. The singles long programs are different with respect to the maximum length (4.5 minutes for men and 4 minutes for women), and the maximum number of jumps (eight for men and seven for women). The ISU has created differences between the ways that men's and women's singles figure skaters compete in the free program that suggest that women figure skaters are less capable than men figure skaters, i.e., they cannot skate for as long or complete as many jumps.

Artistic Gymnastics and Figure Skating are both judged sports on the Olympic programme, as are events in Freestyle Skiing and Snowboarding and Ski Jumping. Judging criteria and/or the application of judging criteria in these events is often explicitly gendered. In the Figure Skating singles events, the ISU uses a different multiplier for the men's and women's scores. The program component scores that men figure skaters earn for the short program are multiplied by 1.0, and for the free skate (long program) by 2.0. Women figure skaters' program component scores are subject to lower multipliers – 0.8 for the short program and 1.6 for the Free Skate.

> According to William Bridel – former national and international competitive figure skater, Director of Athlete Development at Skate Canada from 1997 to 2004, and currently an Assistant Professor in the Faculty of Kinesiology at the University of Calgary – "The opinion is that women's program component scores should be factored to reflect this difference in elements and length of program and, ultimately, ensure an even balance between women's Technical and Program Component Scores in the free program".
>
> *(personal communication, 2014) (in Donnelly et al., 2015).*

However, this rationale does not account for the different multipliers applied to the short program scores because men's and women's short programs are the same length and require the same number of elements. Bridel posits,

> If pressed, the ISU would likely state that the women's Program Component Score is factored in such a way in the Short Program to reflect the

> difference in technical capabilities of men and women. But what it absolutely does is ensure [that] a woman will never outscore a man.
>
> *(personal communication, 2014)*

Further, this artificial differentiation of men's and women's Figure Skating scores ensures that they cannot be accurately compared, and at the Olympic Games, the highest men's scores will always be higher than the highest women's scores.

In Artistic Gymnastics, the FIG determines that men and women gymnasts may earn different scores for performing the same skills. For example, men gymnasts earn a lower score (0.40) for the successful execution of a double salto forward tucked (a tumbling move) on the floor exercise, while women gymnasts executing the same move can earn 0.50. This is based on the assessment of the level of difficulty of the move for the athletes performing it, and indicates that the same skill may be perceived as more difficult to perform for women gymnasts than men gymnasts. There do not appear to be any skills where the reverse is true, i.e., a higher score for difficulty when men gymnasts perform a skill. The FIG also governs Trampoline, which is a judged sport, and the *Code of Points* for Trampoline does not include any explicitly gender-based distinctions in scoring. Men and women athletes' performances are judged using the same criteria in all of the judged Winter Olympic sports, except for Figure Skating.

The slopestyle events in Freestyle Skiing and Snowboarding are judged based on amplitude, execution, variety, progression, combination/flow, and consideration (FIS, 2013). Men and women ride the same course, and the FIS (2013) mandates that "The features and the overall course should be designed in such a manner so as to allow usage by both men and ladies [now, women's] competitors". This mandate intimates that the FIS anticipates that men and women skiers and snowboarders will ride the course differently, and this typically means having multiple 'lines' on the course; paths the athletes can take that vary in difficulty. Halfpipe events in the same sports are judged using almost the same criteria as the slopestyle events: amplitude, difficulty, execution, variety, pipe use, progression, risk taking, combinations, and consideration (FIS, 2013). According to the FIS (2013), "consideration" requires judges to "'know' how difficult tricks and combos are", and to do this

> judges need to have communication with athletes and coaches to see their opinion. This item should be discussed with coaches at official coaches meetings during the season. Not at each competition. Difficulty is very individual and athletes, judges and coaches may disagree with each other when discussing difficulty scales. But judges must have a clear opinion when working on a competition what is easy and what is difficult.

The FIS's recommendations for how to achieve a shared understanding of "difficulty" reveals the ways that judging criteria may be implicitly gendered. Knowing "what is easy and difficult" implies that one group of athletes may earn a different score than another group of athletes for completing the same run in a halfpipe competition. Specifically, men and women skiers and snowboarders may receive different scores for the same tricks and combinations, based on the judges' understanding of how "difficult" they are for that group.

> Snowboarding judge Jeff Elmes confirmed this interpretation of the rules, explaining that judges develop a scoring range for tricks based on their degree of difficulty, which is determined relative to other athletes of the same gender. The tricks that men perform are typically considered by judges to be more difficult, meaning that if a woman and a man performed the identical trick to an identical standard, the woman would receive a higher score; the trick would be considered more difficult relative to what other women competitors are able to perform.
>
> *(personal communication, 2014; in Donnelly et al., 2015)*

BMX freestyle park and Skateboarding street and park events are the most similar sports, in terms of sport culture and judging criteria, at the Summer Games. According to World Skate (2021), the "judging philosophy" for skateboarding includes, "Scoring skateboarding is equal to all genders", and "Skateboard Judging ranks the skater's performance against the current global field of tricks and their execution only". Acknowledging that the skater's gender should not influence how judges score them in Skateboarding seems both commendable and very difficult to achieve. Judged sports require close attention in any assessment of gender equality at the Olympic Games. Specifically, in many cases, the judging criteria for these sports include both explicitly and implicitly gendered elements that cannot be ignored.

Timing

Similar to the Figure Skating singles free program, Boxing, Judo, and Shooting have differentiated between men's and women's events with respect to timing. In Boxing, the International Boxing Association (IBA) decided that men box for three rounds and each round lasts three minutes. Women box for four rounds and each round lasts two minutes, which means that women's boxing matches are one minute shorter than men's matches. In Judo, men's matches last for five minutes, and women's matches last for four minutes. In Shooting, until 2018, the ISSF differentiated between men's and women's events in terms of both the number of shots and the length of time to complete the shots. For example, in both the 10m air pistol and 10m air rifle events at Rio 2016, men took 60 shots in 105 minutes and women took 40 shots in 75 minutes. In January 2018, the ISSF changed the composition of some events to equalize men's and women's number of shots in all Shooting events (an increase to 60 shots for women). Mon-López, Tejero-González, and Calero (2019) claim that this "facilitat[es] (from a methodological point of view) comparison of their [men's and women's] performance", and they assessed the relative performance of men and women shooters before and after the changes. Notably:

> The main finding of this study is that women's pistol and rifle shooting performance did not decline in either case during 2018 as a result of the new regulations introduced by the ISSF in response to the IOC's call for gender equality. The women's average scores during the 2018 European Championship was always similar or higher than their 2016 European Championship scores. Therefore, these regulatory changes have achieved gender equality without detriment to the sporting excellence of women.
>
> *(Mon-López et al., 2019)*

The ISSF is one of the very few IFs that has made changes to the gendered conditions of participation in the organization of their sport at the Olympic Games (as discussed in the previous chapter, most IFs have focused exclusively on the numbers of men and women athletes and men's and women's events), and this has been a successful experience for women shooters, at least in terms of performance. IFs should always include athletes in the decision-making processes about changing the conditions of participation in a sport, and – as discussed with respect to race distances – they cannot assume that it always makes sense to simply change women's events to match the men's events.

Rules of play

There are two sports that have implemented differences in the rules of play for men and women. At the Summer Olympic Games, UWW prohibits women Freestyle wrestlers from performing all double Nelson holds (in the par terre and standing positions), while double Nelson holds are allowed in men's Freestyle Wrestling. It is interesting to have women compete in all elements of a combat sport like Freestyle Wrestling, except for one. If double Nelson holds pose such a significant risk to women wrestlers that they need to be banned, the same is very likely true for men wrestlers. At the Winter Olympic Games, the prohibition of bodychecking in women's Ice Hockey – which the International Ice Hockey Federation (IIHF) introduced after the first women's World Championships in 1990 – differentiates the women's game significantly from the men's full-contact game. It is the most obvious example of 'girls' rules' in a team sport on the Olympic sport programme, that is, women playing a modified version of an already established men's sport using rules that were modified to be more aligned with stereotypical notions of femininity, such as limiting the physical contact between opponents. Making bodychecking illegal does not eliminate body contact altogether, but it is contained to contact that occurs when "there is intent to play the puck first" and incidental collisions. Women's Ice Hockey was added to the Olympic programme in Nagano 1998 (men's Ice Hockey has been played since the first Winter Olympic Games at Antwerp 1920). The IIHF is currently the only IF governing a combat/full contact sport in which the women's game was designed to be so dramatically different than the men's game. The rules of play for men and women in Judo (women's events added at Barcelona 1992), Taekwondo (Sydney 2000), Freestyle Wrestling (Athens 2004), Boxing (London 2012), and Rugby (Rio 2016) are identical (with the exception of the full Nelson holds in Wrestling). It is clearly not the case – either based on the history of women's Ice Hockey and/or the larger context of relatively recently added contact sports on the Olympic programme – that women are not capable of, or uninterested in, playing full contact sports. Conversely, given the increased awareness and understanding of the long-term effects of concussions and traumatic brain injuries in sports such as Ice Hockey, the women's game could potentially serve as a model for all of Ice Hockey.

Protective equipment

The IIHF also differentiates between the protective equipment that men and women hockey players are required to wear. Men players (born after 1979) are required to wear a half face shield and all women players are required to wear a full face shield (e.g., cage or visor). Given that men play Ice Hockey with bodychecking and women do not, it might make sense for men to also wear a full face shield; however, lost teeth and black eyes continue to be perceived as far more appropriate – even celebrated – for men than for women. In Boxing, both men and women boxers were required to wear a headguard at London 2012. Beginning at Rio 2016, the IBF announced that men boxers are not allowed to wear a headguard and that they would review the headguard requirement for all categories. At Tokyo 2020, women boxers were still required to wear a headguard. Women boxers also have the option of wearing a breast protector and a pubic protector. In Fencing, men have the option of wearing a breast/chest protector, and women are required to wear one. In Rugby, only women players may choose to wear chest pads under their jerseys. In each of these cases, additional protective equipment seems like a good idea for everyone, not only for women athletes. Limiting the use of various kinds of protective equipment to women athletes – either as a requirement or an option – perpetuates stereotypical ideas about women being more fragile and needing greater protection than men.

Uniforms

Protective equipment is one small part of one of the most visible and consistent gender-based differences between men's and women's participation at the Olympic Games: uniforms. What men and women athletes are required to wear while they compete at the Games has received increased public attention, and was a popular topic going into Tokyo 2020. Overall, women athletes have challenged attempts to sexualize (or, at least, further gender) their sport participation by, for example, requiring that women badminton players and boxers wear skirts. In both cases, skirts are an option, not a requirement, for women. Further, many women athletes have advocated for the right to wear more modest uniforms, sometimes related to religious and/or cultural expectations of women (e.g., Muslim women athletes wanting to be able to cover their arms and legs, and sometimes also their head and hair), and sometimes related to comfort, confidence, and resisting sexualization (e.g., Germany's women's Artistic Gymnastics team wearing unitards to compete at Tokyo 2020). At the Olympic Games, there are IFs that require different uniforms for women and men athletes, and sports that have optional differences for men's and women's uniforms. When men and women athletes are required to wear different uniforms (as they were in 12 of the 28 sports at Rio 2016), women's uniforms are more revealing – shorter and tighter (e.g., "skin tight", "fitted to the body") – than the men's uniforms. For example, in Trampoline, men are required to wear a "sleeveless or short sleeves singlet, Gym trousers (in a single colour, except black or any other deep dark colour) or Gym shorts". Women are required to wear a "Leotard or unitard with or without sleeves (must be skin tight)" and "Long tights may be worn (must be skin tight and be the same colour as the leotard), any other "dress" which is not skin tight is not allowed". Typically, men's gym trousers or shorts are close fitting, but not "skin tight", nor do the uniform regulations require that they be skin tight. If this was a safety issue, or something that facilitated judging, presumably the requirements for men and women athletes would be the same.[4]

Beach Volleyball receives the most attention for its gendered uniform requirements, and Volleyball (also governed by the FIVB) also mandates significant differences between men's and women's required uniforms. In the gym, the FIVB requires that men's shorts' "waist and length must not be loose or baggy" and the maximum inseam is 10cm. Women's shorts "must fit the body line, tight in waist and length" and the maximum inseam is 5cm or the shorts "must be cut in an upward angle towards the top of the leg". On the beach, men are required to wear a tank top and shorts to play volleyball: "The TANK TOP must fit closely to the body and the design must be with open arms" and "The SHORTS must [...] not be baggy. For all athletes the bottom of the shorts must be a minimum of 10 cm above the top of the knee cap" (FIVB, n.d.). Women are required to wear a bikini or one-piece suit: "The TOP must fit closely to the body and the design must be with deep cutaway armholes on the back, upper chest and stomach (2-piece)" and "The BRIEFS [should] be a close fit and be cut on an upward angle towards the top of the leg". Women beach volleyball players may also wear a "ONE PIECE uniform [that] must closely fit and the design must be with open back and upper chest" (FIVB, n.d.). Following criticism from various outlets ahead of London 2012, the FIVB added "Other Uniform Options and Uniforms for Cold Weather" (cold weather conditions are identified as below 16°C). Each of these options, including a long sleeve top, long pants, and shorts, require that the item "fit closely" and, in the case of the shorts, "the design is recommended to feature total length of 26–28 cm (from waistband) and 26 cm above the knee" (FIVB, n.d.). The FIVB (n.d.) explains how it makes decisions about athletes' uniforms:

> Sun, sand and sea (whenever applicable) are critical elements to take into consideration when it comes to athletes' uniforms. In order to cope with a sunny and sandy environment, the FIVB has established uniform standards [...] based on the recommendations of its medical advisors, athletes, officials and in accordance to the rule 50 (and its By-Law) of the Olympic Charter [...].

This explanation lacks a reasonable justification for how men's and women's significantly different uniforms help them to "cope with a sunny and sandy environment", or why men and women athletes need different uniforms for this environment (or in the gym). It is true that women's Beach Volleyball receives a lot of media coverage during the Olympic Games. Villalon and Weiller-Abels (2018: 1141) found, "As with previous Olympic broadcasts, in the Rio Games, NBC essentially focused on 'socially acceptable' female sports of gymnastics, diving, swimming, track and beach volleyball, during primetime coverage". I do not want to argue that women should not wear bikinis to play Beach Volleyball, but that they should not be required to do so – either because of the FIVB uniform rules or because of a sense that doing so makes them more marketable and media-friendly. Ultimately, athletes – both men and women – should be able to choose what they wear to play without the existing, gendered constraints imposed by IFs that are unrelated to performance or necessity.

At the Winter Olympic Games, men's and women's uniform requirements in Ski Jumping are differentiated with respect to the number and location of seams, as well as the number of pieces used to construct them. The FIS (2013) requires that men's Ski Jumping suits be constructed from five pieces above the waist seam and two below, and women's suits have seven parts for the upper body and eight parts for the lower body.

> Ron Read, a member of the FIS Ski Jumping Committee, explained that until 2011 the uniform regulations were the same for men and women. During that time, Read reported, many women athletes complained about the fit of ski jumping suits for their body shapes. In response to these complaints, the FIS changed the regulations to allow for more comfortable fitting uniforms for women.
>
> (personal communication, *2014*)

The decision to create a different pattern for a women's Ski Jumping suit is aligned with the FIS's consistent requirement – across all disciplines – that men and women skiers and snowboarders wear different-sized starting bibs (worn on the outside of the athlete's uniform with their official number for the competition). That is, for each discipline, the FIS details the specifications for a men's starting bib and a women's starting bib. The men's is always longer and wider at the neck, chest, and waist. The FIS might expand their demonstrated concern about athletes' comfort in their uniforms by considering allowing men and women to choose the suit construction or starting bib that is most comfortable for them, rather than mandating one suit for all men and one for all women.

In Figure Skating, both men and women are required to wear uniforms that are explicitly gendered, particularly in the Ice Dance event. Specifically, men are always required to wear trousers and are not permitted to wear tights. In Singles and Pairs events, women are allowed to wear skirts, trousers, or tights (though it is very rare to see a woman in trousers or tights); and in Ice Dance, women are required to wear skirts. The ISU (2012) requires that all clothing "must be modest, dignified and appropriate for athletic competition – not garish or theatrical in design; must not give the effect of excessive nudity for athletic sport". These requirements enforce traditional beliefs about femininity and masculinity, and those beliefs are further reinforced by the usual size difference of the men and women skating as couples in the Pairs and Ice Dance events, and their gendered roles. The large, "masculine" men lift, throw, and spin the small, "feminine" women. In Figure Skating, as in some sports at the Summer Games, women athletes have more uniform choices than men athletes. That is, while women are allowed to wear skirts and tights, and also trousers ("men's" clothing), men are limited to wearing only trousers in all Figure Skating events. In an effort to achieve gender equality, this might be something the ISU would consider revising.

Many sports do not require different uniforms for men and women athletes, but instead, offer options for athletes' uniforms. Among the optional differences, some are explicitly gendered. For example, only women athletes are allowed to wear skirts or dresses in Archery and Boxing (this means women sometimes have more options than men, i.e., they are able to choose between shorts and a skirt). For example, in Archery, men may wear trousers or shorts, and long or short-sleeved shirts; while women may wear dresses, skirts, divided skirts, shorts or trousers, and blouses or tops. For both men and women, World Archery requires that shorts and skirts "not be shorter than the athlete's fingertips when the arms and fingers are extended at the athlete's side", and that shirts, blouses, or tops "cover the midriff when at full draw". With these rules, men's and women's uniforms are required to have similar coverage of an athlete's body.

Some uniform-related rules are not explicitly gendered, including those in Badminton, Field Hockey, Table Tennis, and Tennis. In these sports, different uniform options are available for athletes (e.g., in Badminton and Field Hockey, athletes may wear shorts or skirts) but it is not explicitly stated that only women may wear skirts. Spectators might be surprised to learn that some sports, such as Field Hockey, have options for men's and women's uniforms because we are so used to seeing gendered uniform differences (e.g., men in shorts and women in skirts on the field). Further, some sports do not identify any gendered differences in uniforms, even though there are apparent and consistent differences in men's and women's uniforms. Most notable is Water Polo, which requires only that "Players shall wear non-transparent costumes or costumes with a separate undergarment". All of the men Water Polo athletes at the Rio 2016 Olympic Games competed wearing traditional brief-style suits, and all of the women athletes competed wearing one-piece suits that covered their chests. The degree of detail provided by various IFs about uniform requirements varies greatly – from the placement of seams on each piece of material used to construct a garment to a list of clothing items from which an athlete may choose. In all cases, athletes need to be involved in making decisions about what they wear to compete, and existing gendered differences need to be reviewed for their necessity, and relevance.

ALL the differences

Within each of the main categories of differences between men's and women's events – length of races; available weight categories (in sports organized by weight classes) and weight limits; height, weight, size, and spacing of equipment used and/or size of the venue; and rules and uniforms – are many subcategories. As demonstrated in this chapter, there are layers of gendered differences composed of multiple examples from a variety of sports and events. Why should we care that in windsurfing (RS-X), the men's mast height is 5.2m and the mainsail area is $9.5m^2$, while the women's mast height is 4.8m and the mainsail area is $8.5m^2$? Viewed on their own, each of these differences may seem trivial. But cumulatively, they demonstrate the continued legacy of the Olympic Games being built on "a foundation of basic meanings about sport predicated on gender differences and distinctions" (Pfister in McLachlan, 2016: 470). They reveal the continued investment on the part of many IFs in emphasizing differences between men and women athletes, to the extent of creating differences in the ways that men and women play the same sports. IFs further accentuate gender difference when they ensure that men's and women's sport performances are not directly comparable. The extent and variation among these gendered differences – these attempts at *within* sport typing – is reminiscent of Mansbridge's concept of "gratuitous gendering". This refers to the application of ideas about gender, and related value judgements, to all parts of our lives. Especially in the context of sex-segregated sport, the implementation of gender differences in all aspects of the ways that athletes play and experience those sports *is* gratuitous.

Larsson (2014) acknowledges that there has been very little discussion in sport about removing gender differentiation: "gender-neutral rules are simply not considered a means to promote gender equality in competitive sport in the same way as they do in other social arenas" (Larsson, 2014: 227). Within sport, gendered differences continue to be normalized and naturalized; they are so commonplace that they can be difficult to identify. Larsson (2014: 227) argues,

> These patterns are, however, chiefly not, at least not among a majority of representatives of the sport organisations, considered to denote inequalities.

> As an expression of neoliberal political discourses, they are rather interpreted as unproblematic choices made by autonomous individuals.

Analysis of these more qualitative inequalities – along with the quantitative inequalities – effectively demonstrates the ways that essentialized and stereotypical understandings of gender continue to influence the composition of the Olympic programme. Assumptions that, for example, all women athletes should use lighter weight equipment (and simultaneously, that all men athletes should use heavier weight equipment) are at odds with acknowledging the diversity of human bodies, and are potentially limiting for all athletes. They are also directly contradicted by the sports on the Olympic programme in which men and women compete using the same equipment.

It is only by applying a more complete definition of gender equality that it is possible to celebrate important gender equality-related accomplishments, without imagining that they are evidence of having achieved gender equality at the Olympic Games. Following McLachlan (2016), it is essential to recognize that the inclusion of women athletes and women's events at the Olympic Games is to be applauded; however, simply being added to the Olympic programme has not led to women's equal participation at the Olympic Games, either qualitatively or quantitatively. Crucially, highlighting the patterns within the gendered differences on the Olympic programme reveals a consistent construction of women's sport as *less than* men's sport. When IFs employ the strategy of *within* sport typing, women's races are shorter, women have fewer weight classes, women use reduced-size equipment and venues, women are required to wear more form-fitting and/or revealing uniforms, and so on when compared to men competing in the same events. This is not a case of offering sport in two categories that have equal status. Rather, "the Olympics and its associated symbols, practices, and texts also reproduce or reinforce the meanings (and accompanying hierarchies) that are assigned to each sex" (McLachlan, 2016: 470). *Within* sport typing perpetuates a hierarchy in which men's sport and men athletes are assumed to be more valuable than women's sport and women athletes.

Making the case that *within* sport typing, in the ways currently represented in sports on the Olympic programme, is an example of gender inequality at the Olympic Games is *not* an argument for gender-integrated competition. In the contemporary sport context globally, girls and women have access to fewer opportunities to participate in sport, and when they do participate, girls' and women's sport continues to be under-resourced compared to boys' and men's sport. This does not provide the necessary foundation to even consider gender-integrated sport at the Olympic Games. Larsson's (2014) reference to "gender-neutral rules" as a means to address existing gendered differences is a possible first step to increased gender equality. In addition, the IOC has advocated for IFs to include mixed-gender events at the Olympic Games, as part of the recommendation to "foster gender equality" (IOC, 2014). Examination of these mixed-gender events reveals that they are often organized in ways that promote gender differences, and it is unclear how mixed-gender events may be used to promote gender equality. This is the focus of the following two chapters.

Notes

1 The IOC's *Gender Equality Review Project* (GERP), conducted in 2018, does address some of the aspects of gender equality included in this chapter. I write more about the GERP in the final chapter.
2 The discussion of gender-based differences in men's and women's participation in sports and events at the Paralympic Games is more than could be accomplished for this book. According to the International Paralympic Committee (IPC, n.d.), the sport-specific classification system "is the cornerstone of the Paralympic Movement", intended to "avoid one-sided and predictable competition, in which the least impaired athlete always wins", by placing athletes in groups based on "the degree of activity limitation resulting from the impairment". This adds even more complexity to the already complex topic of gender difference.
3 Following the Beijing 2022 Olympic Games there has been significant interest in the minimum age requirements for Figure Skating. In June 2022, the ISU decided to increase the minimum age for Figure Skating to 17 years old. This applies to both the men's and women's events.
4 In a number of sports, such as Swimming and Wrestling, there is emphasis on coverage of the chest/breasts for women only, and only women are allowed to wear a two-piece suit for Swimming (in fact, men are not allowed to cover their chests when competing in Swimming).

References

Cervin, Georgia (2015). Gymnasts are not merely circus phenomena: Influences on the development of women's artistic gymnastics during the 1970s. *The International Journal of the History of Sport*, 32(16), 1929–1946.

Cervin, Georgia (2020). Ringing the changes: How the relationship between the international gymnastics federation and the international Olympic committee has shaped gymnastics policy. *Sport History Review*, 51(1), 46–63.

Channon, Anna, Katherine Dashper, Thomas Fletcher & Robert J. Lake (2016). The promises and pitfalls of sex integration in sport and physical culture. *Sport in Society*, 19(8–9), 1111–1124.

Donnelly, Peter & Michele K. Donnelly (2013). *The London 2012 Olympics: A Gender Equality Audit*. Centre for Policy Studies Research Report. Toronto: Centre for Sport Policy Studies, Faculty of Kinesiology and Physical Education, University of Toronto.

Donnelly, Michele K., Mark Norman & Peter Donnelly (2015). *The Sochi 2014 Olympics: A Gender Equality Audit*. Centre for Policy Studies Research Report. Toronto: Centre for Sport Policy Studies, Faculty of Kinesiology and Physical Education, University of Toronto.

FIS (2013/2014). *FIS Freestyle Skiing General Rules for Scoring – Judging Handbook 2013/2014 Edition*.

FIS (22 July 2020). Gender neutral language adopted in all FIS documents. https://www.fis-ski.com/en/international-ski-federation/news-multimedia/news/gender-neutral-language-adopted-in-all-fis-documents. Retrieved: 30 July, 2020.

FIS (18 May 2022). Updates from the Cross-Country Committee Spring meeting 2022. https://www.fis-ski.com/en/cross-country/cross-country-news-multimedia/

news/2021-22/supporting-every-step-of-the-way-coaches-updates-2022. Retrieved: 19 May, 2022.

FIVB (n.d.). Beach Volleyball – Athletes' uniforms guidelines for 2016 Olympic Games. https://docplayer.net/22036832-Beach-volleyball-athletes-uniforms-guidelines-for-2016-olympic-games.html

International Canoe Federation (ICF) (n.d.). The difference between Canoe and Kayak. https://www.canoeicf.com/canoe-kayak-difference.

IOC (2014). *Olympic Agenda 2020: 20 +20 Recommendations*. Lausanne: International Olympic Committee.

IOC (2018). IOC gender equality review project: IOC gender equality recommendations – Overview.

IOC (2021). *Olympic Charter* – In force as from 8 August 2021. https://stillmed.olympics.com/media/Document%20Library/OlympicOrg/General/EN-Olympic-Charter.pdf?_ga=2.69970328.928947499.1654486323-2109730613.1619993075.

IPC (n.d.). What is Classification? https://www.paralympic.org/classification.

ISU (2021). Communication No. 2403 – Summary of results of mail voting on Proposals in replacement of the 58th Ordinary Congress 2021.

Kalinski, Sunčica Delaš; Igor Jelaska & Nikolina Knezević (2017). Age effects among elite male gymnasts. *Acta Kine*, 11(2), 84–89.

Kane, Mary Jo. (1995). Resistance/transformation of the oppositional binary: Exposing sport as a continuum. *Journal of Sport & Social Issues*, 19(2), 191–218.

Kane, Mary Jo & Eldon Snyder (1989). Sport typing: The social "containment" of women in sport. *Arena Review*, 13, 77–96.

Larsson, Hakan (2014). Can gender equality become an encumbrance: The case of sport in the Nordic countries. In Jennifer Hargreaves & Eric Anderson (Eds.), *Routledge Handbook of Sport, Gender and Sexuality* (pp. 226–234). London, New York: Routledge.

Lerner, H.E. (1976). Girls, Ladies, or Women? The Unconscious Dynamics of Language Choice. *Comprehensive Psychiatry*, 17(2), 295–299.

McLachlan, Fiona (2016). Gender politics, the Olympic Games, and Road Cycling: The case for critical history. *The International Journal of the History of Sport*, 33(4), 469–483.

Metheny, Eleanor (1965). *Connotations of Movement in Sport and Dance: A Collection of Speeches about Sport and Dance as Significant Forms of Human Behavior*. Dubuque, Iowa: Wm. C. Brown Company Publishers.

Mon-López, Daniel, Carlos M. Tejero-González & Santiago Calero (2019). Recent changes in women's Olympic shooting and effects in performance. *PLoS ONE*, 14(5): e0216390. https://doi.org/10.1371/journal.pone.0216390

SportBusiness Staff (11 June 2019). Olympic men's tennis final cut to best-of-three sets. https://www.sportbusiness.com/news/olympic-mens-tennis-final-cut-to-best-of-three-sets/. Retrieved: 20 June, 2019.

Teetzel, S. (2009). *A Philosophical Analysis of Olympic Eligibility, Values, and Auxiliary Rules*. Unpublished doctoral thesis, University of Western Ontario, London (Canada).

Theberge, Nancy (1998). "Same Sport, Different Gender": A consideration of binary gender logic and the sport continuum in the case of ice hockey. *Journal of Sport and Social Issues*, 22(2), 183–198.

UNESCO (June, July, August 2015). *Gender Wire – Division for Gender Equality*. No. 1.

United World Wrestling (2022). Disciplines – Olympic styles. https://uww.org/disciplines.

Villalon, Christina & Karen Weiller-Abels (2018). NBC's televised media portrayal of female athletes in the 2016 Rio Summer Olympic Games: A critical feminist view. *Sport in Society*, 21(8), 1137–1157.

Wilson, Wayne (1996). The IOC and the status of women in the Olympic Movement: 1972–1996. *Research Quarterly for Exercise and Sport*, 67(2), 183–192.

World Skate (2021). *Skateboarding Judging Criteria – Olympic Qualification Season 2021.* (Updated on March 10, 2021). http://www.worldskate.org/olympic-qualifying-system/tokyo-2020.html

4

SPORT-SPECIFIC MIXED-GENDER AND OPEN COMPETITION EVENTS AND GENDER EQUALITY

"Encourage the inclusion of mixed-gender team events"

Beginning with *Agenda* 2020, the International Olympic Committee (IOC) has actively promoted mixed-gender events – events in which men and women compete together to earn one medal – as one strategy to "foster gender equality" at the Olympic Games. Specifically, in Recommendation 11, the IOC (2014) committed to "encourage the inclusion of mixed-gender team events". Many International Federations (IF) adopted this strategy and proposed mixed-gender events for inclusion on the programmes at the Olympic Games beginning with Sochi 2014. At each subsequent edition of the Games, the number of mixed-gender events increased.

At the Summer Olympic Games, the number of mixed-gender events increased from eight at London 2012 (mixed doubles Badminton[1] and Tennis[2] and six Equestrian events) to nine at Rio 2016 (with the addition of one Sailing event) and doubled to 18 at Tokyo 2020 (with the addition of one mixed-gender event in each of Archery, Athletics, Judo, Swimming, Table Tennis, and Triathlon, and three events in Shooting). The approved programme for Paris 2024 includes an additional four mixed-gender events (an additional event in Athletics and three in Sailing) for a total of 22.

At the Winter Olympic Games, three mixed-gender events were included at Vancouver 2010 (Figure Skating pairs and ice dance, and Luge doubles – officially a mixed event, but only men competed), three mixed-gender events were introduced at Sochi 2014 (with the addition of one mixed-gender event each in Biathlon, Figure Skating, and Luge), and the total number of mixed-gender events increased to eight at Pyeongchang 2018 (one mixed-gender event in Alpine Skiing and one in Curling). The approved programme for Beijing 2022 includes an additional four mixed-gender events (one mixed-gender event each in Freestyle Skiing, Ski Jumping, Snowboarding, and Short Track Speed Skating) for a total of 12 mixed-gender events.

DOI: 10.4324/9781003002741-4

The success of this strategy is undisputed; the IOC has effectively encouraged the IFs to include mixed-gender events in a variety of individual and team, and summer and winter, sports. However, it is unclear how – and if – the inclusion of mixed-gender events contributes to gender equality at the Olympic Games. In this and the following chapter, I introduce and provide examples of the categories of mixed-gender events on the Olympic programme, and attempt to unpack both the intention and the reality of mixed-gender events as a tool to promote gender equality at the Olympic Games.

Throughout these chapters, I use the term "mixed-gender" and its companion terms "single gender" and "gender-segregated" because "mixed-gender", or often only "mixed", is the term used by the IOC and the IFs. It would be more accurate to refer to "mixed-sex" or "sex-integrated" events and "single sex" or "sex-segregated" events, because the Olympic programme is organized using binary sex categories (male and female) and these categories continue to be assumed to be biologically determined.

Mixed-gender events: four categories

There are four broad categories of mixed-gender events included on the Olympic programme: relay events; team events; sport-specific events; and open competition events. I have developed these categories for the purposes of description and analysis; they are not used by the IFs or the IOC. I have used the IFs' language with respect to mixed-gender relay, team, and open competitions. With the exception of open competition events, teams competing in mixed-gender events are required to include at least one man and one woman. At the Olympic Games, the athletes must represent the same country, though this is not always the case at the Youth Olympic Games. According to the IOC, mixed-gender events are "a sign of innovation",

> While men and women compete separately in some combined team events, in several others they go head-to-head in direct competition. Mixed events are an exciting spectacle and often unpredictable, thrilling to the end for both the competitors and fans.
>
> *(IOC, 2018)*

Among and within the four categories of mixed-gender events, there is much variation in the ways the events are organized, as well as when the events were invented and/or introduced at the Games. For example, events such as mixed doubles Tennis have long histories (first included on the Olympic programme at Paris in 1900). There is also significant overlap among the categories with respect to the characteristics evident in the practice, organization, and reality of mixed-gender events.

Mixed doubles Curling is one of the most recent additions to the Olympic programme (the World Curling Federation (WCF) held the first World Mixed

Doubles Curling Championship in 2008, and mixed doubles Curling debuted at the Winter Olympic Games at Pyeongchang in 2018). Most mixed-gender events are contested by athletes who also compete in the equivalent segregated men's or women's events. One exception is mixed doubles Badminton, where the competitors seem to be specialized players (i.e., there is little or no crossover between the athletes in the men's doubles and women's doubles events, and the athletes competing in the mixed doubles event). Other than Badminton and Sailing, mixed-gender events offer IFs the opportunity to increase their number of medal events on the Olympic programme, without increasing their athlete quota numbers. Mixed-gender events, then, allow IFs to explicitly meet Recommendation 11 of the IOC's *Agenda 2020* recommendations – to increase the number of events for women (and, by definition, for men as well) – while implicitly meeting the requirement of Recommendation 9 – to maintain or, preferably, reduce the overall number of athletes at the Games. Despite this, the relationship between mixed-gender events and gender equality is not obvious. This is apparent following a detailed analysis of specific events in each of the four categories.

A note about counting events

Before exploring the four categories, it is important to understand how the IOC has used mixed-gender events to do some 'creative counting' of the number of women's events at each edition of the Olympic Games. The IOC produces a "Factsheet – Women in the Olympic Movement" that has been updated approximately every two years since at least 2016. Each factsheet includes two tables: "Women's participation in the Games of the Olympiad" and "Women's participation in the Olympic Winter Games". Each table shows the number of sports and events for women, and the percentage of the total events that were women's events, as well as the total number of women athletes and the percentage of all athletes they represent, at every Olympic Games to date. The relevance of this document to a discussion of mixed-gender events lies in one small asterisk that appears after the column titled "Women's events*", and is explained as "*including mixed and open events" (IOC, 2020). This means that beginning with women's participation in the Paris 1900 Games, the IOC has counted mixed-gender and open events *only* as women's events. Mixed doubles Tennis is counted as a women's event, in spite of each competing team being composed of one man and one woman. It is more accurate to count mixed gender doubles events as 0.5 of an event for men and 0.5 of an event for women. The Luge mixed gender relay event, which includes one men's singles sled, one women's singles sled, and one doubles sled, provides opportunities for three men athletes and one woman athlete. It is more accurate to count this event as 0.75 of an event for men and 0.25 of an event for women; yet, like all mixed-gender events, the IOC counts the Luge mixed-gender relay event as a women's event. Open events – in which both men and women are allowed to compete – in sports such as Equestrian, Sailing, and Shooting have been counted as women's events even when no women competed in them (they simply were not barred from competing by the ruleset). I raise this issue of creative counting here for two purposes: (1) It sheds some light on the connection the IOC makes between mixed-gender sports and gender equality. That is, when the IOC counts mixed-gender events only as women's events, they artificially inflate the number of women's events on previous Olympic programmes, and promote those programmes and the Olympics generally, as being more gender equal than they actually are. (2) This creative counting obscures the reality of mixed-gender events, that is, the requirement that both men and women compete in an event (this is the case with all mixed-gender events added post-2010). As you read about the types of mixed-gender events included on the Olympic programme, keep in mind that the IOC until very recently has counted each one of these events *only* as a women's event.

The most recent version of the "Factsheet – Women in the Olympic Movement" was published in December 2021 (IOC, 2021). For the first time, the IOC reported two separate numbers of events: (1) Women's only events; and (2) Mixed events; and then reported the percentage of women's only events (of the total number of events at each Games), and the percentage of women's/mixed events. This change is significant in terms of acknowledging that mixed-gender events are not interchangeable with women's events, and thus warrant reporting as a separate category. At the same time, by including mixed-gender events in their reporting about women's involvement at the Olympic Games, and particularly sharing a combined percentage of women's and mixed-gender events as a proportion of all events at each edition of the Games, the IOC promotes the narrative that mixed-gender events are for women and/or contribute to gender equality. This, in spite of the fact that mixed-gender events offer at least as many opportunities for men athletes as for women athletes.

In this chapter, I introduce and discuss sport-specific mixed-gender events and open competition events. These are the categories of mixed-gender events that have the longest histories on the Olympic programme. Specifically, events in these two categories were included at both Summer and Winter Olympic Games before the release of *Agenda 2020*, and the IOC's more recent concerted effort to include more mixed-gender events as part of the commitment to increasing gender equality at the Games. In the next chapter, I focus on the categories of mixed-gender events – relay and team – that compose the majority of mixed-gender events that have been added to the Olympic programme by IFs since *Agenda 2020*.

Mixed-gender sport-specific events

The category of mixed-gender sport-specific events encompasses primarily established events on the Olympic programme (e.g., mixed doubles events in Badminton and Tennis, Figure Skating ice dance and pairs events), and a small number of recently introduced events (e.g., mixed doubles Curling, the Nacra-17 event in Sailing). These events include many of the characteristics shared by all mixed-gender events, with the exception of open competition events. Prominent among these characteristics is mixed-gender events' existence as an additional medal event in a sport that does not require additional athletes. For example, mixed gender doubles Tennis relies on men and women athletes who have already qualified for either the singles or gender-segregated doubles events (this is a requirement of the event). Mixed gender doubles Badminton; however, seems to be a more specialized event, with little crossover between the athletes in this event and the single-gender Badminton events. At Rio 2016, 27 athletes competed only in the mixed doubles event, and five athletes (three men, two women) competed in the mixed gender and single gender doubles events. A mixed gender Tennis event was contested at the Olympic Games from 1900 to 1924, but it was not until London 2012 that a mixed doubles event was re-introduced to the Olympic programme.

The Summer Olympic Games have featured a Badminton mixed doubles event since Atlanta 1996. The International Tennis Federation's (ITF) decision to return mixed doubles to the Olympic programme was likely heavily influenced by the opportunity to add a medal event without needing to increase the number of Tennis athletes, and also promoting greater use of the Tennis facility. A third mixed gender doubles event – in Table Tennis – has been added to the Summer Olympic Games for Tokyo 2020. Mixed doubles is a long-standing event in Table Tennis; it has been contested at the International Table Tennis Federation (ITTF) World Championships since 1926. However, it has taken 32 years (since Table Tennis was added to the Olympic programme at Beijing 1988) for the addition of a mixed gender doubles event. The athlete quota for Table Tennis has not increased to account for the mixed doubles event, and the mixed doubles event uses the same facility as the single-gender events. ITTF President, Thomas Weikert, suggested that adding this event was a reward for Table Tennis: "The ITTF is extremely happy to have Mixed Doubles added to the Olympic Program. Table Tennis obtained very high television and social media numbers at Rio 2016, so we feel that a fifth gold medal was deserved" (ITTF, 2017).

This demonstrates that there are many factors involved in decision-making about the Olympic programme (e.g., the popularity of the sport), not only – or even predominantly – gender equality. Mixed-gender doubles events, and particularly mixed doubles Tennis, are central to these (predominantly racquet) sports. It is possible that the language of "mixed-gender events" is derived from the "mixed doubles" event in Tennis (a sport that receives significant media attention globally outside of the Olympic Games because the players are well known from the professional tennis tours). And, it explains the frequent shortening of "mixed gender" to simply "mixed" events; even when "mixed" (on its own) could refer to many things, that is, it is not at all specific to gender.

The Winter Olympic Games include some of the most established mixed-gender events and one of the newest. The Figure Skating pairs event – that features couples composed of one man and woman – debuted on the Olympic programme at London 1908 and has been a mainstay since Antwerp 1920. Ice dance was added at Innsbruck 1976. In these events, the man and woman are integrally involved in an incredibly physically demanding program (routine) that is intended to tell a story, convey emotion, meet the technical requirements of the event (e.g., jumps, lifts) and – perhaps most importantly – appear effortless. In addition, due to the rules and expectations established by the International Skating Union (ISU), men and women perform stereotypically gendered roles; men lift, throw, spin, and otherwise appear to manipulate their women partners' bodies – but not vice versa. Beginning at Pyeongchang 2018, a mixed (gender) doubles Curling event joined the existing mixed-gender events in Figure Skating at the Winter Olympic Games.

Demonstrating the similarities across the categories of mixed-gender events (discussed further in the next chapter), the mixed-gender event in Curling includes fewer athletes than the single-gender event; like Archery and Badminton, whose single-gender team events include three athletes and mixed-gender team events include only two athletes. Single-gender Curling teams are composed of four athletes, while mixed doubles Curling is exactly as it sounds – one man and one woman who take turns throwing the stones. According to Hutchins (2018), mixed doubles Curling's "virtues start with an inherent emphases [sic] on equality: mixed doubles puts team members and genders on even footing in terms of both influence over the game and public recognition" (Hutchins, 2018). Like the smaller team events in Archery and Badminton, the WCF has emphasized that it is possible for more countries to compete in mixed doubles Curling. According to WCF president, Kate Caithness:

> You just have to look at some of the teams who have won medals at the World Mixed Doubles Curling Championship over the past few years - the likes of Hungary, Spain and Austria for example. They are associations that are improving year on year, particularly in Mixed Doubles, but find it difficult to break through in Traditional Curling competitions. Now that this discipline will be part of the Games, many more associations will have a chance of winning an Olympic medal.
>
> *(in WCF, 2015)*

In 2019, "In the largest mixed doubles field in world curling history, 48 teams [competed]. In fact, five teams are making their world curling championship debuts — Kosovo, Nigeria, Saudi Arabia, Ukraine and Mexico" (Heroux, 2019). Curling is distinct from Archery, Badminton, Shooting, etc. (which require athletes to have qualified for a single-gender event in order to compete in a mixed-gender event) in that the WCF allows the National Curling Federations to determine if athletes are eligible to compete in both the single-gender and mixed doubles events.

Some national federations, such as Curling Canada, restrict athletes' participation to either the single-gender or mixed doubles event; while others, such as the

Swedish Curling Association allow athletes to compete in both. Canadian curler, John Morris, has advocated for Curling Canada to change its policy, claiming,

> What they're [Scotland, Sweden] doing now, and I believe is a good, proactive approach, is giving their country the best chance at multiple curling medals by opening mixed doubles to all of the curlers in their country, no matter if you qualify in the men's and women's.
>
> *(in Houston, 2020)*

Rather than increasing the opportunities for athletes (men and women) at the Olympic Games, the majority of mixed-gender events on the Olympic programme encourage and/or (most often) require athletes to 'double up' in single and mixed-gender events. Having athletes compete in multiple events helps to achieve the IOC's goal of controlling the size of the Games, but it is not clear how it helps to promote gender equality.

Fewer athletes competing in more events, especially with different teams/partners, also raises specific concerns. For example, Curling Canada national coach and programme manager for men's and mixed doubles, Jeff Stoughton, believes the single-gender and mixed doubles teams should remain separate:

> "We just feel, at this time, the cons outweigh the pros," Stoughton said. Under the current schedule, mixed doubles players miss the four-player team practice on both days, with the start of the team competition coinciding with the media day for mixed doubles. "Basically, you'd have not seen your team for the last two weeks," adds Stoughton. "We just don't think it's that great for the team. It's great for the mixed doubles player but you've got to look at all the emotions that are involved too. If you win the gold medal, you're ecstatic and excited and you want to let loose but you have to play the next day and for the next week and a half. That's a big grind to have that huge emotional outburst and then have to come back down to earth".
>
> *(in Houston, 2020)*

Notably, athletes in mixed-gender events in other sports (and in single-gender relay and team events) manage to prepare for and compete in multiple events, despite their outcomes. Like mixed doubles Badminton, mixed doubles Curling has been a specialist event, that is, there are athletes who compete exclusively in mixed doubles Curling; however, many mixed doubles athletes also compete in single-gender events (on teams of four throwing eight stones in ten ends).

According to *The Rules of Curling*, in mixed doubles curling,

> Each team shall deliver 5 stones per end. The player delivering the team's first stone of the end must also deliver the team's last stone of that end. The other team member shall deliver the team's second, third and fourth

> stones for that end. The player delivering the first stone can change from end to end.
>
> *(World Curling Federation, 2020)*

Each team determines which athlete (man or woman) will throw first and last (two stones), and which athlete will throw the second, third, and fourth stones (three stones) in each of eight ends. The medal games at Pyeongchang 2018 revealed gendered patterns in these decisions. For example, in the gold medal game between Canada and Switzerland, the women team members threw the first and last stones and the men threw the second, third, and fourth stones. This means that over six ends, each woman threw 12 stones, and each man threw 18 stones. During the broadcast of the bronze medal game on the Olympic Channel, one commentator confirmed this was the pattern for all teams, with one exception: "The OAR [Olympic Athletes from Russia][3] is the only team that played their line-up with the man throwing one and five. All the other teams had their woman throwing one and five with the guys throwing two, three, four", and "You definitely need a hard thrower in the two, three, and four spot in your line-up with those stones". The second commentator responded, "Clearly it works for them" (Olympic Channel, 2018). It seems that no team alternated the player delivering the first stone between ends. The player responsible for the first and last shots

> must have excellent draw skills, and will rarely throw heavy weight hit shots. The 2-3-4 player will often be called upon to throw heavy weight clearing shots as well as precision draws [...] Male players can usually throw heavier weight accurate shots.
>
> *(personal communication, 2020)*

Matt Hamilton, who represented the United States in mixed doubles at Pyeongchang 2018 echoes this belief, "If the other team has a couple of rocks in the rings [scoring position], generally the male curler is going to be able to move more granite, so to speak, and throw a little harder" (in Clarke, 2018). Presumed differences between men's and women's abilities are reinforced by the official "Shot success percentage" record from the Gangneung Curling Centre (Pyeonchang 2018), which is divided by gender, despite this being a mixed-gender event. Mixed doubles Curling reinforces the premise that even when men and women compete together in a way that has the potential to realize the 'promise' of sex integrated sport, that is, a man and woman athlete composing a team, working together, doing the same activities (throwing the stones, sweeping), and wearing the same uniform, traditional ideas about essential gender differences (e.g., men are stronger than women) are still very much at play.

In December 2020, the International Paralympic Committee announced that a mixed gender doubles Wheelchair Curling event will debut at the Milan Cortina 2026 Winter Paralympic Games. This was an early announcement about the programme, and all medal events and athlete quotas will be confirmed in late 2022/early 2023. About this decision, Morgan (2020) claims, "The IPC Governing Board has provisionally approved the first 18 medal events – all of which are for women – for the first time 'in order to give National Paralympic Committees (NPCs) and International Federations additional time to plan for the Games'."

It seems that the IPC, like the IOC, also categorizes mixed-gender events as "for women", even though they are also "for men". The IPC's Women in Sport Committee Chairperson, Rita van Driel, said, "We would like to see more mixed events. Curling is a mixed event and it doesn't make a difference if you are a man or woman" (in Bates, 2018). As demonstrated by the discussion of the mixed doubles Curling event at the Olympic Games, this is not entirely true. In fact, the mixed doubles event in Wheelchair Curling builds on the already existing team event, which is also mixed gender. Each four-person team must include at least one woman. This is an interesting version of "mixed-gender", one that requires women's representation on the team, but not women's equal representation. In other ways, Wheelchair Curling is similar to Curling; it uses the same ice surface and stones, though there is no sweeping.

Confirmation of the mixed gender doubles event for the Paralympic Games in Milan Cortina 2026 requires that the WCF meet the following conditions: "(1) A reduction of teams in the Mixed Team event from 12 to 10—a reduction of 10 athlete quota slots" and "(2) Inclusion of no more than eight Mixed Doubles teams—an increase of 16 athlete quota slots" (World Curling Federation, 2020). This results in an overall increase of six athlete quota places for Wheelchair Curling. This is noteworthy given the strict guidelines for Olympic sport IFs to add mixed-gender events without increasing their required athlete quota. Concerns about the size of the Games are a greater issue for the Olympic Games (over 11,000 athletes at Rio 2016 and almost 3,000 athletes at Pyeongchang 2018) than they are for the Paralympic Games (over 4,000 athletes at Rio 2016 and under 600 athletes at Pyeongchang 2018). Of particular interest are the claims acknowledging that the mixed gender and women's events that have been provisionally added to the Milan Cortina 2026 programme are not already established events. For example, IPC President, Parsons, explained, "We strongly believe the provisional inclusion of medal events will facilitate participation growth, advancing the possibilities of them meeting the criteria for inclusion when the medal events programme is fully confirmed in two years' time" (in Morgan, 2020). And, IPC Athletes' Council chairperson, Chelsey Gotell, maintained, "With more than five years to go until the Games, athletes, national and international federations, as well as NPCs have a target to aim for in terms of developing the talent pool" (in Morgan, 2020). Like some of the previously discussed mixed-gender events (e.g., the team events in Shooting), the mixed-gender doubles Curling event has been developed for the purposes of demonstrating gender equality by increasing the number of "women's events" on the Paralympic programme. While these events provide equal opportunities for men's participation, they also potentially take the place of mixed gender and/or women's events that could develop more organically.

Sailing has an incredible number of disciplines and events to choose from when it proposes the events to be included on the Olympic programme; World Sailing recognizes over 100 Class Associations, each with multiple events. At Rio 2016, World Sailing introduced a mixed-gender event in the Nacra 17 class. According to the World Sailing *Racing Rules of Sailing*, for the mixed-gender event, "The crew shall consist of one female person and one male person". The Nacra 17 event (and a women's laser radial event) replaced men's and women's keelboat events. World Sailing tested six boats to select the boat for this new multihull mixed-gender event at Rio 2016, and the Nacra 17 was the most popular among the sailors and the evaluation committee. Consideration of the mixed-gender organization of the event is apparent in some of the evaluations; one sailor claimed, "For me this is the Olympic boat. [...] It has good loads that are enough to make the boat athletic but still allow for crew rotation between male and female", and a member of the evaluation panel wrote: "Good size for mixed sailing, crew weight OK, loads OK, either man or woman as crew or helm" (in ISAF, 2012). The rules, and based on the evaluations, the boat itself, do not dictate what role – skipper or crew – the 'female person' on the crew shall play; however, among the 20 teams that competed at Rio 2016, 16 had the man as the skipper and the woman as the crew (2016 Olympic results). Luke Ramsay and Nikola Girke represented Canada in the Nacra 17 event at Rio 2016. According to Ramsay,

> But the initial thinking [about crew position] was that it would be smarter to have a male crew who was really strong, really fit, pulling from another [class of] boat [...], and then have a female driver who could do a little more finesse. However, interestingly, a lot of the fleet has actually gone the other way. I think one of the reasons for that is the catamaran [multihull] experience in the world was pretty much male dominated. [...] I think that's one of the reasons why we saw a spike in how well the male drivers are doing, but now I think the fleet might be evening out a little more as the female drivers start to figure things out. Over the years, it's sort of balancing itself out in the top ten.
>
> *(in Luke Ramsay: Catamaran Convert, 2016)*

The idea of the man as "really strong, really fit" and the woman working with "a little more finesse" sounds a lot like the gendered explanations for line-up decisions in mixed gender doubles Curling (heavy weight versus precision). It is notable that men have been overrepresented in the skipper or driver role, despite these beliefs about 'natural' gendered abilities making men better suited to the crew role.

The Nacra 17 event is the first time in the history of Sailing at the Olympic Games that a mixed-gender event has required the participation of both men and women. According to the Olympic Studies Centre (2017b), all Sailing events from Paris 1900 (when Sailing was added to the Olympic programme) until Los Angeles 1984 were "mixed". Beginning in 1988, Sailing events were divided into men's, women's, and mixed-gender categories. At the Olympic Games from 1900 until London 2012, Sailing events categorized as mixed-gender had been open to both men and women; however, the vast majority of athletes were men. That is, an event can be categorized as mixed-gender, even if no women participated. For example, at Beijing 2008, the 49er class event was one of three mixed-gender (the IOC designation) or "open" (the World Sailing designation) events. Nineteen teams, composed of two athletes each, competed in the 49er event, and all 38 athletes were men (2008 Beijing Olympic Sailing Competition). In the mixed-gender Finn class event, all 26 athletes were men, and Carolijn Brouwer was the only woman among 30 athletes (15 teams) who competed in the mixed-gender Tornado class event (2008 Beijing Olympic Sailing Competition). In these cases, mixed-gender events – and, particularly, counting mixed-gender events as women's events – is terribly misleading if not dishonest. At London 2012, the Sailing programme included six men's events and four women's events. This is the only Olympic Games at which there were no mixed-gender or open events, and with the addition of the Nacra 17 event at Rio 2016 and three additional mixed-gender events at Paris 2024 (replacing both men's and women's single-gender events), London may be the only Games ever to have no mixed-gender Sailing events. Sailing is an example of what we might consider the return to mixed-gender events. That is, mixed-gender – more commonly referred to as open – events were historically part of the Olympic programme; however, as demonstrated by Sailing, these events were often mixed-gender in name only.

Open competition

Equestrian is the only remaining open competition sport on the Olympic programme. Both historically and currently, "open" indicates that both men and women athletes are able to participate, or, more accurately, that women are not excluded from participation in events that are generally recognized as men's events. The current use of "mixed-gender" requires participation by athletes of both genders, that is, that men and women from the same country compete together (in some capacity) in the event. According to de Haan et al. (2016), "in the context of equestrian sport, there are no sex-based biological advantages for either males of females"; and "the relevance of the rider's sex is unimportant in Olympic equestrian sport, as it is the physical performance of the horse, rather than the human athlete who is judged" (1250, 1251). Three disciplines of Equestrian: dressage, eventing, and show jumping are included on the Olympic programme, with an individual and team event in each discipline. This is a total of six medal events that the IOC has counted as women's events, even though there is no requirement that women participate in them. Women were excluded from participation in Equestrian at the Olympic Games from the sport's inclusion at

Paris 1900 until Helsinki 1952. "In 1952, women were allowed to compete only in Dressage; in 1956, Showjumping was opened to female competitors; and in 1964, they were finally allowed to compete in the military-dominated Eventing competition" (de Haan et al., 2016: 1250). de Haan et al. (2016: 1250) note that "men and women have however always competed against each other in Para-Equestrian Dressage [the only Para-Equestrian discipline], since its inclusion in the 1996 Atlanta Games".

Women's and men's contemporary participation numbers reflect the gradual inclusion of women in the Olympic Equestrian disciplines. Dumbell and de Haan (2012) studied the gender composition of athletes over 50 years of Olympic Games Equestrian events and found that women's participation has increased dramatically, but not consistently across the three disciplines:

> women were most likely to be competing in Dressage both then and now, but they now form a much greater proportion with 55% of competitors at recent games being female. [...] Showjumping, however, is still heavily dominated by male competitors with only 17% of athletes at recent games being female, although this has grown since the meagre 3% in earlier games. Finally, Eventing has seen the largest growth from no female competitors to 33% of the competing athletes now being female.
>
> *(in de Haan et al., 2016: 1253)*

Women are overrepresented in dressage compared to the other Olympic disciplines. Hedenborg and White (2012) explain that this is likely "due to the fact that Dressage riding was more compatible with an accepted femininity" (in de Haan et al., 2016: 1253). Dressage is a judged event during which the rider prompts the horse to perform a series of pre-determined moves. It is commonly described in artistic terms. For example, "Dressage, the highest expression of horse training, is considered the art of equestrian sport" (olympic.org) and "Dressage is the ultimate expression of horse training and elegance. Often compared to ballet, the intense connection between both human and equine athletes is a thing of beauty to behold" (fei.org). In this sense, dressage is closely connected to other judged Olympic sports that emphasize graceful, expressive performances most often associated with dominant understandings of femininity, such as Gymnastics and Figure Skating. Women's overrepresentation in dressage illustrates Dashper's (2012: 217) assertion that "There are no explicit, formal barriers to participation for girls and women at any level of equestrian sport, but this does not ensure equality of opportunity". Open competition, like the other categories of mixed-gender events, does not necessarily contribute to gender equality; more attention is needed to the organization and details of these events before they can be celebrated unconditionally for promoting gender equality.

Channon et al. (2016: 1113) claim, "when women and men compete against each other on equal terms, as happens in equestrian sport at all levels, it becomes apparent that specific aspects of athletic performance are not fundamentally rooted in sex difference". At the same time, Dashper (2013) found that men are disproportionately represented among the top Equestrian riders relative to their overall numbers among Equestrian riders.

> This suggests that desegregation alone does not go far enough to overcome the longstanding and persistent marginalisation and subordination of women in sport and even in a sport where men do not have any biophysical advantage. As this study suggests, merely allowing women to compete against men in equestrian sport has done little to redress gender inequality because of the subtle but powerful gender negotiations that operate at a less visible level.
>
> *(Dashper, 2012: 223)*

Dashper is particularly focused on the social, cultural, and economic factors that influence gender relations – interpersonally and institutionally – and continued gender inequality. These factors are what challenge the reality of "women and men competing against each other *on equal terms*". Institutionally, "equal terms" are not provided by the most recently added mixed-gender Olympic events. Instead, they replicate the gender differences that already exist within the sport. That is, many mixed-gender events are organized in ways that reveal and promote assumptions about "natural" gender differences by building these assumptions into the structure of the event. Determining what it means to compete on equal terms, as well as a clear sense of how to define gender equality, are missing from Recommendation 11, and particularly from the endorsement of mixed-gender events as a means to promote gender equality on the Olympic programme.

On the Paralympic programme, there are a few team sports that are 'open' to participation by men and women. Wheelchair Rugby became a full medal sport at the Sydney 2000 Paralympic Games. The International Paralympic Committee (IPC) describes Wheelchair Rugby as "a mixed-team sport for male and female athletes. Players compete in manual wheelchairs specifically designed for the sport. Players must meet minimum disability criteria and be classifiable under the sport classification rules" (paralympic.org). The sport is full-contact and combines elements of rugby, basketball, and handball. Each team has four athletes on the court, and those athletes are assigned to one of

> seven classes ranging from 0.5 to 3.5 with functional characteristics identified for each athlete class. In general, the 0.5 class includes those athletes with the most disability and the 3.5 class includes those athletes with the least disability or "minimal" disability eligible for the sport of wheelchair rugby.
>
> *(IWRF, n.d.)*

The sum of the classification points of a team's players – on the court at one time – may not exceed eight. The Canadian Paralympic Committee (CPC) claims, "This ensures teams play a mix of athletes with a range of functional levels" (paralympic.ca). Coaches strategically consider their players' classification points when they decide which players to field and in what roles. For example,

> A team could play one 3.5 player as the primary ball carrier, a 2.5 player to assist the ball carrier in passing and scoring, and a 1.5 and 0.5 player to block and hold opposing players who are trying to defend.
>
> *(IWRF, 2012)*

According to Article 35 of the International Wheelchair Rugby Federation (IWRF) rules, teams are allowed additional points for putting women athletes on the court: "For each female player on the court a team will be allowed an extra 0.5 points over and above the 8 points for the team" (IWRF, 2019). According to the CPC, this makes women players "increasingly valuable players to recruit in to [sic] the sport" (paralympic.ca). Among the top five teams at Rio 2016, only Canada and Great Britain each included one woman athlete on their teams. Australia, Japan, and the United States sent teams composed exclusively of men athletes, and won the gold, bronze, and silver medals respectively. It is possible to view the additional 0.5 classification points for women athletes as an incentive to recruit and play women athletes. This seems like a positive decision by the IWRF to encourage teams at all levels of Wheelchair Rugby to include women athletes. However, it is also possible to understand the additional 0.5 classification points for women athletes as a suggestion that women athletes are further 'disabled' simply by being women in Wheelchair Rugby. That is, when a woman is on the court, a team needs more athletes in the 'least disability' classifications. Sailors (2016: 1135) asserts, "equality through sex integration will require more than good intentions and a coherent theory so long as cultural ideas about male superiority persist". Like its Olympic counterparts, the organization of Wheelchair Rugby as an open sport – with no regulatory barriers to women's participation – does not mean women's equal participation.

Para Ice Hockey (also called Sledge Hockey) is, arguably, Wheelchair Rugby's winter equivalent.

> Para Ice Hockey is the Paralympic sport version of ice hockey. All players have a lower body impairment and are strapped to a two-bladed sledge. They propel themselves with sticks spiked at one end and curved blades at the other for shooting.
>
> *(paralympic.ca)*

The sport's debut at Lillehammer 1994 featured one woman athlete, Bri Mjaasund Oejen of Norway; "The rules were more relaxed then, allowing the sport to focus on participation" (Syal, 2018). Then, until Vancouver 2010, Para Ice Hockey was designated as a men's only sport. According to Smith and Wrynn (2014), the IPC announced that women could be included on teams for 2010, but no women played Para Ice Hockey in Vancouver. Nor did any women play at Sochi 2014. At Pyeongchang 2018, Lena Schroeder of Norway became the second woman ever to compete in Para Ice Hockey at the Paralympic Games. Canada, the United States, Great Britain, and Europe (composed of athletes from five countries) have national women's Para Ice Hockey teams, and the World Para Ice Hockey Federation (WPIHF) is planning to hold the first women's World Championships in 2021 (Women's Para Hockey Féminin, 2020). Syal (2018) claims, "having women play along with the men is not the endgame for the Canadian women's team. They're aiming to become their own Paralympic sport by 2022". This suggests that for many women Para Ice Hockey players, undeniably limited access to participation in an open category is not as appealing as playing on women's teams in women's competitions, including at the Paralympic Games.

How can we explain men's dominance in the open competition of both Para Ice Hockey and Wheelchair Rugby at the Paralympic Games? Part of the explanation is the significant disparity between men's and women's participation at the Paralympic Games in general. Houghton et al. (2018: 11) found that "There were 133 female athletes (23.6%) and 431 male athletes (76.4%) [at Pyeongchang 2018], compared with 129 female athletes (23.8%) and 412 male athletes (76.2%) in 2014, and 121 female athletes (24.1%) and 381 male athletes (75.9%) in 2010". Smith and Wrynn (2014: 60) identify a number of potential explanations for this disparity:

> One on-going contention is that more males than females have spinal cord injuries, and more men are injured in war, thus there is a larger population of men than of women to draw from (Shackelford, Farley, and Vines, 1998). However, the Paralympic Games include athletes with a variety of other disabilities that do not have such discrepancies between males and females. Female Paralympians also face stereotypes that focus on their perceived fragility, more than is the case for males, as well as facing challenges about appearing feminine while being athletic.

Most relevant to this discussion about mixed-gender events is the recognition that open events often offer less in terms of promoting gender equality than do the more recently added mixed-gender events that require the participation of men and women athletes from the same country (discussed in the next chapter). Open events are certainly preferable when there is no women's event on the Paralympic programme, such as in Para Ice Hockey and Wheelchair Rugby. This is something that might be considered for the Olympic programme, that is, re-categorizing men-only sports such as Baseball and Nordic Combined as open sports, in which women may participate. However, this should not be an opportunity for the IOC (or IPC) to count those events as women's events, especially when no women participate in them. At the same time, it behooves the IPC, WPIHF, and IWRF to identify and address the conditions that serve to limit women's participation so severely.

As discussed previously in the cases of Sailing and Shooting, the open category is not static, and changes over the past 40 years or so have resulted in events that were previously open (allowing the participation of both men and women) becoming single-gender or mixed-gender (requiring the participation of both men and women). The Luge doubles event is an excellent example of an event undergoing this transition. According to the IOC, "in 1964, luge made its Olympic debut, at the Innsbruck Games, with a mixed event, a men's event and a women's event. The programme has not changed since then" (olympic.org). The mixed-gender Luge event is the doubles event (two athletes on one sled) and though it has technically been an open event, only men have competed in the doubles event at the Olympic Games. This causes some confusion about how to discuss Luge doubles. For example, Pavitt (2020) claims, "At present, only men's doubles is part of the flagship tour alongside the men's and women's singles and the team relay. This is mirrored at the Winter Olympics to date". Specifically, an open (or mixed-gender) event in which only men compete is widely understood as a men's event. This general understanding – and practice – of Luge doubles as a men's event has recently been codified with the introduction of women's doubles events. The Fédération Internationale de Luge de Course (FIL) effectively proposed the inclusion of a women's doubles event at the Youth Olympic Games at Lausanne 2020, and based on the success of that event, applied for the inclusion of a women's doubles event at Beijing 2022. That application was unsuccessful, and the FIL has again proposed the inclusion of a women's doubles event for Milan Cortina 2026. After the first women's team competed in a World Cup men's doubles race in December 2019 (Star wire services, 2019), FIL has added a women's doubles event to the World Cup schedule beginning in the 2021/2022 season (FIL, 2020). Recognition that Luge doubles has realistically been a men's event is further highlighted in the claim that "Efforts to develop women's doubles have followed IOC demands for gender equality across all of its sports" (Pavitt, 2020). Further, the FIL has changed the maximum weight for the athlete pair from 180kg for the "doubles general class" (the open event) to 150kg for the women's doubles event (FIL, 2020). This mirrors the gendered weight regulations that exist in the men's and women's singles events; the maximum weight for men is 90kg and for women is 75kg. The introduction of a women's doubles event means there are genuine opportunities for women to compete in Luge doubles, and at the same time, it reinforces the idea of natural differences between men and women (with respect to weight and ability) by seeming to conclude that women cannot compete in an open category.

Conclusion

Exploring the ways that mixed-gender events have been organized as part of the Olympic programme – and, especially those events in the sport-specific and open competition categories – reveals the primary complication of associating mixed-gender events and gender equality. Specifically, "encourag[ing] the inclusion of mixed-gender team events" as a strategy to "foster gender equality" at the Olympic Games requires the uncritical acceptance that a mixed-gender event, by virtue of including both men and women, is gender equal (IOC, 2014). As detailed in this chapter, and further explored in the following chapter, it is apparent that more thoughtful, careful consideration of the organization, structure, and promotion of – as well as the reporting about – mixed-gender events is needed to ensure that mixed-gender events are in a position to actually "foster gender equality".

Notes

1 According to the Olympic Studies Centre, mixed doubles Badminton was introduced to the Olympic programme at Atlanta 1996, after Badminton became a full medal sport at Barcelona 1992 (IOC, 2017a).
2 According to the Olympic Studies Centre, one mixed gender Tennis event was included on the programme at the Paris 1900 Olympic Games, two mixed gender events at Stockholm 1912, one mixed gender event each at the Antwerp 1920 and Paris 1924 Olympic Games. Tennis was removed from the Olympic programme after 1924, and did not return until Seoul 1988. A mixed gender doubles event was reintroduced at London 2012 (IOC, 2015).
3 Alexander Krushelnitsky and Anastasia Bryzgalova won the bronze medal game. However, Krushelnitsky tested positive for the banned substance meldonium at the Games and the team was stripped of their win. Krushelnitsky was banned from Curling for four years (CBC Sports, 2018).

References

2008 Beijing Olympic Sailing Competition (n.d). https://site-isaf.soticcloud.net/2008-olympic-games.php?rgtaid=9689&evntid=16200&view=fleetevent&includeref=regattapageresults31821#results__9689. Retrieved: 17 February 2021.

Bates, Charlotte (13 March 2018). The rise of women at Paralympic Games. https://news.cgtn.com/news/3263444d796b7a6333566d54/share_p.html. Retrieved: 16 February, 2021.

CBC Sports (4 December 2018). Russian curler banned for 4 years in Olympic doping case. https://www.cbc.ca/sports/olympics/winter/curling/doping-alexander-krushelnitsky-banned-4-years-1.4932384. Retrieved: 4 March, 2021.

Channon, Anna, Katherine Dashper, Thomas Fletcher & Robert J. Lake (2016). The promises and pitfalls of sex integration in sport and physical culture. *Sport in Society*, 19(8–9), 1111–1124.

Clarke, Liz (8 February, 2018). In Olympic curling, men and women are not created equal. *Washington Post*.

Dashper, Katherine (2012). Together, yet still not equal? Sex integration in equestrian sport. *Asia-Pacific Journal of Health, Sport and Physical Education*, 3(3), 213–225.

de Haan, Donna, Popi Sotiriadou & Ian Henry (2016). The lived experience of sex-integrated sport and the construction of athlete identity within the Olympic and Paralympic equestrian disciplines. *Sport in Society*, 19(8–9), 1249–1266.

Heroux, Devin (19 April 2019). 48 teams, only 1 champion: Canada itching for elusive mixed doubles world curling title. https://www.cbc.ca/sports/olympics/curling/world-mixed-doubles-curling-preview-canada-1.5105170. Retrieved: 27 January, 2021.

Houghton, E.J., Pieper, L.P., & Smith, M.M. (2018). *Women in the 2018 Olympic and Paralympic Winter Games: An Analysis of Participation*, Leadership, and Media Coverage. New York, NY: Women's Sports Foundation.

Houston, Michael (20 March 2020). Morris urges Curling Canada to change Olympic eligibility rules. https://www.insidethegames.biz/articles/1092172/john-morris-curling-canada-olympics. Retrieved: 23 March, 2020.

Hutchins, Aaron (13 February 2018). Pyeongchang 2018: Why mixed doubles curling deserves to stay in the Olympics. https://www.macleans.ca/olympics/pyeongchang-2018-why-mixed-doubles-curling-deserves-to-stay-in-the-olympics/. Retrieved: 17 February, 2021.

IOC (2014). *Olympic Agenda 2020: 20 +20 Recommendations*. Lausanne: International Olympic Committee.

IOC (March 2015). TENNIS: History of Tennis at the Olympic Games. Olympic Studies Centre. https://stillmed.olympic.org/AssetsDocs/OSC%20Section/pdf/QR_sports_summer/Sports_Olympiques_tennis_eng.pdf

IOC (2017a). BADMINTON: History of Badminton at the Olympic Games. Olympic Studies Centre. https://stillmed.olympic.org/media/Document%20Library/OlympicOrg/Factsheets-Reference-Documents/Games/OG/History-of-sports/Reference-document-Badminton-History-at-the-OG.pdf

IOC (2017b). SAILING: History of Sailing at the Olympic Games. Olympic Studies Centre. https://stillmed.olympic.org/media/Document%20Library/OlympicOrg/Factsheets-Reference-Documents/Games/OG/History-of-sports/Reference-document-Sailing-History-at-the-OG.pdf

IOC (19 September 2018). Mixed-gender events a sign of innovation at the Youth Olympic Games. https://www.olympic.org/news/mixed-gender-events-a-sign-of-innovation-at-the-youth-olympic-games. Retrieved: 19 December, 2020.

IOC (June 2020). Factsheet – Women in the Olympic Movement. https://stillmed.olympics.com/media/Documents/Olympic-Movement/Factsheets/Women-in-the-Olympic-Movement.pdf

IOC (December 2021). Factsheet – Women in the Olympic Movement. https://stillmed.olympics.com/media/Documents/Olympic-Movement/Factsheets/Women-in-the-Olympic-Movement.pdf

ISAF (21 April 2012). 2016 Mixed Multihull - Panel report and recommendations. https://www.sail-world.com/Australia/2016-Mixed-Multihull-Panel-report-and-recommendations/-96329?source=google. Retrieved: 17 February, 2021.

ITTF (9 June 2017). Table Tennis mixed doubles added to Tokyo 2020 (Press release). https://www.ittf.com/2017/06/09/table-tennis-mixed-doubles-added-tokyo-2020/. Retrieved: 13 January, 2021.

IWRF (n.d.). A laypersons guide to Wheelchair Rugby classification. https://iwrf.com/?page=classification. Retrieved: 27 January, 2021.

IWRF (2012). Wheelchair rugby – Sequence of events. https://iwrf.com/resources/iwrf_docs/Wheelchair_Rugby_Game_Sequence_2012.pdf. Retrieved: 27 January, 2021.

Luke Ramsay: Catamaran Convert (13 March 2016). https://www.sailingscuttlebutt.com/2016/03/13/luke-ramsay-catamaran-convert/. Retrieved: 17 February, 2021.

Morgan, Liam (16 December 2020). Mixed doubles wheelchair curling and two women's snowboard events added to Milan Cortina 2020 Winter Paralympic programme. https://www.insidethegames.biz/articles/1102062/ipc-milan-cortina-2026-paralympics. Retrieved: 18 December, 2020.

Olympic Channel (13 February 2018). *OR v OAR (Bronze Medal) – Mixed Doubles Curling | PyeongChang 2018 Replays* [Video]. Olympic Channel. https://www.olympicchannel.com/en/video/detail/nor-v-oar-bronze-medal-mixed-doubles-curling-pyeongchang-2018-replays/.

Pavitt, Michael (26 July 2020). FIL applies for natural track and women's doubles luge inclusion at Milan Cortina 2026. https://www.insidethegames.biz/articles/1096692/-luge-natural-track-doubles-milan-cortina. Retrieved: 28 August, 2020.

Sailors, Pam R. (2016). Off the beaten path: Should women compete against men? *Sport in Society*, 19(8–9), 1125–1137.

Smith, Maureen M. and Alison M. Wrynn (2014). History of gender and gender equality in the Olympics and Paralympics. In Jennifer Hargreaves & Eric Anderson (Eds.), *Routledge Handbook of Sport, Gender and Sexuality* (pp. 57–65). London, New York: Routledge.

Star wire services (December 2019). Canadian lugers Caitlin Nash and Natalie Corless become the first female team to compete in a World Cup doubles race. https://www.thestar.com/sports/2019/12/14/canadian-lugers-caitlin-nash-and-natalie-corless-become-the-first-female-team-to-compete-in-a-world-cup-doubles-race.html. Retrieved: 20 February, 2021.

Syal, Richa (6 March 2018). Canadian women's sledge hockey team fights for the right to play. https://www.theglobeandmail.com/sports/olympics/canadian-womens-sledge-hockey-paralympics/article38213587/. Retrieved: 20 February, 2021.

Women's Para Hockey Féminin (9 February 2020). The world is on notice: The women of winter are coming. https://www.wphcanada.com/news. Retrieved: 20 February, 2021.

World Curling Federation (October 2020). R.16 Mixed doubles curling. *The Rules of Curling – and Rules of Competition*. https://s3.eu-west-1.amazonaws.com/media.worldcurling.org/media.worldcurling.org/wcf_worldcurling/2021/10/11092643/2021-The-Rules-of-Curling.pdf

5

MIXED-GENDER RELAY AND TEAM EVENTS AND GENDER EQUALITY

"Encourage the inclusion of mixed-gender team events"

Beginning with the Sochi 2014 Winter Olympic Games, the International Olympic Committee (IOC) has promoted the inclusion of mixed-gender events on the Olympic programme as part of its commitment to improving gender equality at the Olympic Games. These are the Games held after the approval and publication of *Agenda 2020*, which includes Recommendation 11: "Foster gender equality", and one of two strategies to achieve it: "Encourage the inclusion of mixed-gender team events" (IOC, 2014). Although the programmes for Sochi 2014 and Rio 2016 were decided before *Agenda 2020* was released, some International Federations (IFs) were already using mixed-gender events to increase their total number of medals at the Games, without needing to ask the IOC for additional athlete quota places. Both the mixed-gender relay in Biathlon and the mixed-gender team event in Figure Skating debuted at Sochi 2014, and these mixed-gender events served as a model for other IFs in the development and proposal of their own mixed-gender events for the Olympic programme.

In this chapter, I continue to explore if, and how, mixed-gender events contribute to improving (or fostering) gender equality at the Olympic Games. The focus is on the two remaining categories of mixed-gender events: relay events; and team events (sport-specific mixed-gender events and open competition events are the focus of the previous chapter). Again, I have developed these categories for the purposes of description and analysis; they are not used by the IFs or the IOC. The majority of mixed-gender events added to the Olympic programme since *Agenda 2020* fit into one of these two categories; some of these events look very similar, if not identical, to single-gender events in the same sport (e.g., Archery, Shooting). Others, such as the mixed-gender relay in Triathlon require athletes to train for a very different kind of competition (a sprint event) at the same time that they prepare for their single-gender Olympic events. These events further demonstrate that mixed-gender events are not necessarily gender

DOI: 10.4324/9781003002741-5

equal – in many cases, they replicate gender differences that exist in a sport's single-gender events, and/or introduce new issues related to gender, such as taking gender into account when determining the order of athletes competing on a relay team. In the latter case, gender differences and inequalities – emphasizing women athletes' lesser performances relative to men in the same sport – are reinforced, not eliminated, or even reduced.

Mixed-gender relay events

Among the first mixed-gender events added to the Winter Olympic programme post-*Agenda 2020* is the mixed-gender relay event in Biathlon. Biathlon combines cross-country skiing and rifle shooting (from prone and standing positions). It was originally introduced as an Olympic demonstration event in an earlier form (military patrol) in 1924 and became a medal event for men at Squaw Valley in 1960. Women's Biathlon events were added to the Olympic programme at Albertville in 1992 (https://www.olympic.org/biathlon-equipment-and-history).

The length of time on the Olympic programme is not the only difference between men's and women's Biathlon. Women compete over shorter distances than men (e.g., 15km versus 20km in the individual event, 7.5km versus 10km in the sprint, 10km versus 12.5km in the pursuit), and women's courses have lower minimum and maximum 'climb values' than men for each loop and for the competition (e.g., 400m minimum and 600m maximum total climb per competition in the individual event for women versus 550m minimum and 800m maximum for men) (IBU, 2020). Despite the difference in race distances, women and men incur the same penalties for missing targets during the shooting bouts; 45 seconds time added in the individual events or an added 150m penalty loop in all other events (IBU, 2020). The specifications for the rifle are the same for all athletes with respect to calibre, trigger resistance, weight, and other elements. This differs significantly from the equipment requirements for the rifle events in Shooting at the Summer Olympic Games before 2018. For example, in the 50m rifle 3 positions event, women's rifles were required to weigh 6.5kg and men's rifles were required to weigh 8kg. In Biathlon, the specifications for men's and women's skis and poles are the same, or they are determined by the height of the athlete. According to the *International Biathlon Union (IBU) Event and Competition Rules* (Annex A), "Minimum ski length is the competitor's height minus 10cm" and "The maximum length of the poles must not be longer than the competitor's body height" (IBU, 2020, pp. 7–8). These are the same requirements as those for skis and poles in Cross Country Skiing. Both men and women compete in Biathlon relay events that include four athletes who each ski and shoot at 2km and 4km (one time from the prone position and one time standing). Athletes in the men's relay each ski 7.5km, and athletes in the women's relay each ski 6km (IBU, 2020).

These gendered differences in race distance are consistent with some other Olympic sports (e.g., Alpine Skiing, Cycling); however, as noted previously, there are many sports in which women and men athletes compete over the same distances, and on the same tracks or courses – including some of the longest Olympic races (e.g., the marathon in Athletics, the open water event in Swimming, Triathlon). It could be argued that it makes sense to maintain the gendered differences in distance that exist between the men's and women's Biathlon competitions when designing the mixed-gender relay event. That is, athletes train to compete over this distance. Like many mixed-gender events, the Biathlon mixed relay is not a specialist event, i.e., the competitors compete primarily in single-gender individual and relay events.

However, not all IFs have incorporated differences in race distance in their mixed-gender relay events, even when this may be possible. For example, the Luge mixed-gender relay includes one men's singles athlete, one women's singles athlete, and one doubles team. Results are determined by adding together the times of each relay team's three 'legs' (and the shortest time wins). There are a number of gendered differences in Luge, including different course distance and elevation for men's and women's events (men's tend to be longer and higher) and weight allowance (the maximum body weight allowed for men Luge athletes is 90kg (117kg with sled), and for women is 75kg (102kg with sled). And, although the doubles event has traditionally been labelled by the Fédération Internationale de Luge de Course (FIL) as a mixed-gender event, typically only men have participated in this event. This fact is reinforced by the FIL's recent introduction of a women's doubles event. That means the Luge mixed-gender relay event has been contested by teams composed of three men and one woman.

Even with the overrepresentation of men in the mixed-gender relay, all sleds use the same starting point, which is the 'women's' starting point during the singles events. This is noted here for two main reasons: (1) Unlike the Biathlon mixed-gender relay, the comparable event in Luge has the men's singles athletes competing over a different (shorter) distance than during the singles competition. This suggests that the men competing in mixed-gender relays do not inevitably need to replicate the distance they compete in during their single-gender events. This highlights the decision-making – and lack of uniformity in decision-making – among the IFs with respect to mixed-gender events. (2) Having men's singles athletes 'move down' to a lower starting point to compete in the mixed-gender relay suggests both that men are able to compete over shorter distances and that women are not able to compete over longer distances. The continued implication of women's lesser abilities in mixed-gender events seriously calls into question their ability to 'foster gender equality' on the Olympic programme.

The Biathlon mixed relay made its Olympic debut at Sochi 2014, as one of three newly added mixed-gender events. In April 2011, the IOC announced the inclusion of these events, and women's Ski Jumping (ultimately, 12 new events were approved for inclusion at Sochi 2014 – four men's events, five women's events, and three mixed-gender events). In the IOC press release, then president, Jacques Rogge, is quoted as saying: "These are exciting, entertaining events that perfectly complement the existing events on the sports programme, bring added appeal and increase the number of women participating at the Games" (IOC,

2011). Even before the adoption of *Agenda 2020* (in 2014), the IOC's promotion of mixed-gender events was connected to claims about increasing women's participation at the Olympic Games, though this is never explicitly explained, and the evidence presented below suggests this is not actually the case.

Biathlon's mixed-gender relay has been contested at the World Biathlon Championships since 2005. The IBU explains,

> As the name says, the mixed relay is a mixed-gender competition, formed with teams of two women and two men. The competition specifics are, in principle the same as in the regular relays. Women compete over 6 km, men over 7.5 km.
>
> *(IBU, 2017)*

Initially, the IBU also dictated the starting order of athletes and required that it be "female, female, male, male". This meant that men athletes always finished the race and received the spectator and media attention that accompanies crossing the finish line. Thus, the IBU succeeded in creating a mixed-gender event in which the men and women athletes remain as separate (and as differentiated) as possible.

The structure of the mixed-gender relay is completely at odds with an academic understanding of mixed-gender – or gender-integrated – sport. According to Channon et al. (2016: 1112),

> In its simplest form, the fundamental 'promise' of sex integration lies in the fact that it challenges us to reject a priori assumptions of male superiority and to entertain a very different vision of sex difference and gender relations to those typically constructed through traditional models of gendered physical culture. When women and men face each other as ostensible equals in athletic contests, when they train with one another in ways which are taken to be mutually beneficial, or when they rely on one another's athletic prowess for the sake of team success, the usual gendered logic stressing inevitable male predominance stands to be challenged.

Choosing to have men and women race over different distances, and particularly, to have women race over a shorter distance than the men on their team, in the same event, reinforces assumptions of "male superiority" and "male predominance". By dictating the order of competition, and ensuring that women and men do not compete "head to head", the IBU further avoids the possibility of "women and men fac[ing] each other as ostensible equals".

With the exception of the second woman biathlete tagging her man teammate in a transition, men and women are not even on the course at the same time. The IBU emphasized this intentional separation of men and women athletes (who are competing as a team in a mixed-gender event) in 2018. At the IBU Congress, the IBU decided to institute more flexibility for the single mixed relay (explained below) and mixed relays. Specifically, they approved the option of men going first during the mixed-gender relay events. The Technical Committee for an event now determines if the men or women will start the race. In its press release, the IBU clarified this option: "**Important note:** This still means that it will be *either* women first *or* men first – this decision will be made in advance, meaning men and women will not be competing on the same leg" (IBU, 2018, emphasis in the original). Adding this option to the mixed-gender relays means that women biathletes will sometimes have the opportunity to cross the finish line, and receive the corresponding media and fan attention. However, it further institutionalizes the separation of the men's and women's competitions – even within a mixed-gender event.

In 2016, the IBU announced the addition of a single mixed relay event to its World Championships starting in 2019. A single mixed relay team is composed of one man who skis 7.5km and one woman who skis 6km, both on the same 1.5km loop. IBU president, Anders Besseberg, claimed, "IBU is also proud to be the first international winter sport federation to have introduced mixed events on the highest competition level, and we fully understand that others are following our success of developing mixed gender teams" (IBU maintains mixed gender drive, 2016). It is concerning that other IFs may have looked to Biathlon for a mixed-gender event model to emulate; particularly because this model replicates and reinforces gender differences in men's and women's participation. That is, even when competing as a team, in the same event, men's and women's participation is differentiated – and women's participation is potentially minimized – by having women compete over shorter distances. At Beijing 2022, the mixed-gender relay in Biathlon was modified so that each athlete skied 6km (notably, the "women's distance"), which may make it better suited to being a model for other mixed-gender events.

It is not the case that all mixed-gender relay events differentiate the men's and women's distances, and especially those included on the programme for the first time at the Tokyo 2020 Summer Olympic Games. In sports such as Athletics, Swimming, and Triathlon, men and women relay teammates will compete over identical distances on/in the same track, pool, or course. A 4 × 400m mixed-gender relay on the track and a 4 × 100m mixed-gender medley relay in the pool are the first mixed-gender events for the two largest sports at the Summer Games. Notably, the 4 × 100m mixed gender medley relay in Swimming has already been included on the programme for the Youth Olympic Games:

> A relay quartet comprises two men and two women, and the teams can determine in what order the athletes compete, with the medley relay comprising all four strokes, starting with backstroke before breaststroke and butterfly, with freestyle the anchor leg.
>
> *(IOC, 2018)*

The same will be true of the event at Tokyo 2020. This approach, which dictates the order of styles but not the order of athletes, seems to move closer to the "promise" of mixed-gender sport. World Athletics has not dictated the order of athletes for the 4 × 400m relay. In both Athletics and Swimming, unlike the Biathlon and Luge mixed-gender relays, there is the potential to see men and women competing against each other directly, i.e., on the track or in the pool at the same time. Allowing athletes to compete in the position/style in which they are strongest, rather than using gender to determine the starting order looks more like gender equality.

The Tokyo 2020 Paralympic Games will also feature the first mixed-gender relay events in Athletics and Swimming. Specifically, a mixed gender and class 4 × 100m relay will be contested on the track:

> It will see athletes from the various different classifications compete side-by-side. Each team is comprised of two men and two women. They must include a representative from the T11–13 vision impairment class, one from either the T33–34 or T51–54 wheelchair racing classes, one from the T35–38 co-ordination impairment classes, and an athlete with a limb impairment from the T42–47 or T61–64 classes.
>
> *(Morgan, 2018)*

And, two mixed-gender 4 × 100m freestyle relay events will be contested in the pool, one for athletes with a vision impairment and one for athletes with an intellectual impairment. Mixed-gender events are not as atypical on the Paralympic programme as they have been on the Olympic programme; many Paralympic sports include some kind of mixed-gender event (e.g., a mixed-gender double scull event in Rowing, a number of open events discussed below). Arguably, this is related to a historical emphasis on participation at the Paralympic Games that has not been a feature of the Olympic Games. International Paralympic Committee (IPC) President, Andrew Parsons, when discussing the Tokyo 2020 programme, raised a point that some Olympic sports have also used to justify the inclusion of mixed-gender events: "The addition of mixed gender relays will also enable more countries to participate" (in Morgan, 2018). Notably, the mixed-gender relay in Athletics is also open to athletes who have different (specified) classifications. However, with mixed-gender relay events, countries need to have only two qualified men athletes and two qualified women athletes to field a relay team, unlike single-gender relay events that require four qualified athletes of one gender. Mixed-gender relay – and other – events may mean more opportunities to win a medal for smaller countries.

According to International Triathlon Union (ITU) president, Marisol Casado, Triathlon's mixed-gender relay event moves closer to the "promise" of mixed-gender sport, at least in terms of "when [men and women] rely on one another's athletic prowess for the sake of team success, the usual gendered logic stressing inevitable male predominance stands to be challenged" (Channon et al., 2016: 1112). This event, which will be contested for the first time at Tokyo 2020, includes two men and two women competing in a "super-sprint triathlon consisting of a 300-meter swim, 7-kilometer bike and 1.7K run with the fastest combined time winning" (Price, 2019).

The mixed-gender relay event is the only relay event in Triathlon. Unlike many other mixed-gender events, which replicate the single-gender event, the ITU has created a very different event as its mixed-gender offering. The implications of this for athletes and training are addressed below. When announcing the launch of the ITU's Mixed Relay Series. Casado said,

> The mixed relay is an event that gives the sport something very important: a sense of team building. But most important, is an event that demonstrates that women and men can compete together but both are equally important to the success of the team. And I am sure that all those teams will shine brightly in Nottingham for the debut of the Series.
>
> *(ITU launches Mixed Relay Series, 2017).*

Interestingly, the ITU, which otherwise has a strong track record with respect to gender equality in their events, has chosen to mandate the order of athletes by gender: woman, man, woman, man. Like the original plan for the Biathlon mixed-gender relay, this ensures that men always receive the spectator and media attention associated with crossing the finish line and, ultimately, winning the race. Alongside race distance, the starting order of athletes in mixed-gender relay events requires attention if these events continue to be promoted as improving gender equality on the Olympic programme.

Based on the examples discussed in this section, it is apparent that not all mixed-gender relay events are created equal, and not all mixed-gender relay events contribute to gender equality. Rather, as Channon et al. (2016: 1114) state, "many aspects of how integrated sports are organized refuse the possibility that women might ever compete on a 'level playing field' with men". It seems that, in general, IFs whose established events are more gender equal develop mixed-gender (relay) events that are also more gender equal. The Biathlon versus Triathlon comparison effectively illustrates the ways that existing gendered differences – which are unequal – in a sport's single-gender events can be replicated in their mixed-gender events, or not when there are no or few differences in their gender-segregated events. To date, there is not an example of gender differences having been introduced for an IF's mixed-gender event, but these differences are often reproduced, rather than addressed or eliminated. Together, these issues challenge the ways in which mixed-gender events might serve to foster gender equality. Further, they demonstrate that mixed-gender events may actually raise new issues with respect to gender equality rather than automatically achieve gender equality (e.g., such as the gender order of athletes in an event).

Strategy associated with choosing the order of athletes (including a consideration of gender) is new with the introduction of mixed-gender relay events for which the IF has not mandated the athlete starting order. An IOC news post

(2019) emphasized the importance of "tactics" in the debut of the 4 × 400m relay event at the World Athletics Championships in 2019:

> The other strategic aspect of this new event is [the first is choosing which athletes to include], of course, deciding the order in which the athletes will run, bearing in mind that, on average, men are approximately six seconds quicker than women over the distance (44–45 seconds for men compared to 50–51 seconds for women). All options are possible: two men followed by two women, or the other way round, or alternating between men and women. Most teams opted to begin with a man, followed by two women, with a man then running the anchor leg.

When athletes' gender becomes part of the discussion about strategy in a mixed-gender event, it serves to emphasize, rather than disregard (or minimize or celebrate), gender differences. And, when those differences are framed, as they are by the IOC news post, to highlight women's performances as a potential deficit to their team, i.e., their slower times must be strategically accounted for, gender inequality is perpetuated. That is, instead of contributing to greater gender equality, this approach reproduces the beliefs inherent in "coercively" gender-segregated competition; that – due to essential, natural differences – women cannot compete directly with men and be successful. According to Channon et al.,

> in many contexts, the potential for transformative experiences in sex-integrated sports is thwarted or at least slowed by the persistence of deep, historically rooted and often taken-for-granted practices which marginalize women, [and] rationalize the ascendancy of men into positions of authority.
>
> *(2016: 1114)*

Mixed-gender relays and other events are not able to effectively foster gender equality when they operate within the same sport culture that continues to value men's sport and athletes more than women's. Instead, they will – as demonstrated – simply raise new issues, such as gender as strategy, and the reproduction of gender differences.

Mixed-gender team events

The reproduction of existing gender differences is especially apparent in the mixed-gender team events on the Olympic programme. In many mixed-gender team events, men and women athletes compete with each other as a team in the most nominal way. That is, their scores are added together to calculate a total team score; however, their actual competition looks almost identical to a single gender event, as detailed in the following examples.

Mixed gender team events are a relatively recent phenomenon, beginning with the International Skating Union's (ISU) introduction of a Figure Skating team event at Sochi 2014. This team event includes one men's singles skater, one ladies' (the official ISU designation as of January 2021) singles skater, one ice dance couple, and one pairs couple; all athletes must qualify for their primary competition (singles, ice dance, pairs) in order to compete for their country in the team event. Every one of the many gender differences that are institutionalized in Figure Skating is reproduced in the team event. This includes gendered uniform requirements in singles, ice dance, and pairs, as well as differences between men's and women's singles in the duration of the free program, scoring, required elements, and number of jumps. In an event that is promoted as contributing to gender equality, women skate a shorter free program (four minutes maximum compared to the men's four and half minutes), women's scores are multiplied by a lower number (0.8 short program and 1.6 free skate for women, and 1.0 short program and 2.0 free skate for men), and women are limited to seven jumps "for a well-balanced program" while men are allowed to perform eight jumps (for details, see Chapter 3). Further, women are allowed to wear skirts, tights, or trousers (though, most commonly, they wear skirts), while men are required to wear trousers and are explicitly prohibited from wearing tights. The Figure Skating team event, rather than having "women and men face each other as ostensible equals", reproduces gendered differences between men and women figure skaters. In addition, although the athletes in the team event do depend on their teammates to perform well and earn high scores, it is not apparent to the audience that the men and women "rely on one another's athletic prowess for the sake of team success" (Channon et al., 2016: 1112) – beyond the stereotypically gendered partnerships of the man and woman skaters composing each ice dance and pairs couple. The same is true of the Alpine Skiing parallel slalom team event, i.e., athletes compete separately (men versus men and women versus women), and their times are combined for one total team time. Like Figure Skating's team event, the outcome is determined by adding together the results of essentially single-gender competitions. Beyond the IOC's decision to count mixed-gender events as women's events, how do events organized in this way work to foster genuine gender equality on the Olympic programme?

Tokyo 2020 featured the first mixed-gender team events added to the programme for the Summer Olympic Games. These included events in Archery, Judo, and Shooting. In Judo, three men judokas and three women judokas competed as a team in the mixed-gender team event. There are seven weight categories each for men and women on the Olympic programme; however, the International Judo Federation (IJF) elected to include only three men's weight categories (73kg, 90kg, +90kg) and three women's weight categories (57kg, 70kg, +70kg) in the team event. To field a full team, countries were able to enter an athlete in a higher weight category than they had qualified to compete in at the Games (e.g., a women's 48kg judoka could compete in the 57kg category if a country did not have a judoka qualified for the Games in the 57kg category).

Both Archery and Shooting introduced mixed-gender team events composed of only two athletes, one man, and one woman.

Much like the Winter Olympic sports, the mixed-gender team events in the Summer sports reproduce any existing gender differences between men's and women's competition. In Judo, differences include weight categories and uniform requirements (women must wear a white t-shirt under their judogi). In the Shooting mixed team 10m air pistol and 10m air rifle events, both the man and woman take 40 shots which, until 2018, was the number of shots in the qualifying round of women's air pistol and air rifle events. Since 2018, both men and women take 60 shots in the qualifying rounds. Each of these mixed-gender team events – in Archery, Judo, Shooting, Alpine Skiing and Figure Skating – is an example of indirect competition: "In direct competition the performance of one athlete affects that of another, as in football and basketball; in indirect competition, each athlete competes against the course or clock, as in bowling and golf, rather than any other athlete" (Sailors, 2016: 74). Sailors (2016) claims that indirect competition is better suited to being organized in mixed, versus gender-segregated, events.

However, the organization of these mixed-gender team events disrupts the seemingly apparent distinction between direct and indirect competition identified by Sailors (2016). It is true that Figure Skating and Judo athletes compete to be awarded the judges' highest scores, parallel slalom Alpine skiers compete to have the fastest time, and Archery and Shooting athletes compete to score the highest number of points and, as such, seem to meet the criterion of indirect competition. However, at the same time, mixed-gender team event athletes are engaged in direct competition – against other athletes – as they do so. This is most apparent in Judo, with two athletes fighting each other on the mat, and also in Alpine Skiing's parallel slalom event, with two athletes racing each other on courses parallel to one another on the same hill. In both of these mixed-gender team events, women athletes compete directly against women athletes and men athletes compete directly against men athletes. Each round of competition in the Judo mixed team event consists of six individual bouts (one in each weight category). According to Ney Wilson Pereira, the High Performance Manager of the Brazilian Judo Confederation, this combination of individual events "will give the Olympic programme gender equality, offering the same opportunities to and creating a climate of integration between the male and female team. I think it brings a much more favourable climate" (What is the new judo mixed team event? 2020). Similarly, in Alpine Skiing's mixed-gender parallel slalom team event, each round of competition consists of four races between athletes from the same two teams. The Fédération Internationale de Ski (FIS) has determined a fixed athlete starting order based on gender: woman, man, woman, man. Like the mixed-gender relay events with similar imposed starting orders, this ensures that a man from each team will always have the opportunity to not only win their individual race, but also win the heat for their team (each team earns one point for a win). The consistent claims that mixed-gender events promote gender equality seem to be based more on the idea of women and men comprising one team for an event, than they are about the actual organization of the event.

In the Shooting mixed team trap event, men shoot first and women shoot second; though, in the case of a shoot off (due to a tie), the team decides who shoots first. In the mixed team air rifle and air pistol events, the teams decide which athlete shoots first and athletes arrange themselves accordingly (the athlete on the left for each team shoots first). Teams also determine their own shooting order in the Archery mixed team event. World Archery Secretary General, Tom Dielen, emphasized this point: the mixed-gender team event is

> a way of showing that in our sport there's not much difference between men and women, and it's a quick and entertaining event to add to the programme. [...] It's up to the team to decide what they want to do, who shoots when – that's part of the tactics.
>
> *(in Stanley, 2017)*

The reference to selecting the order of athletes as "tactics" echoes the points made about the Athletics and Swimming mixed-gender relay events. That is, it is necessary to take into account the athletes' gender when determining the running, swimming, or shooting order for the event. Instead of emphasizing gender equality, considering an athlete's gender as part of the strategic planning for a mixed-gender event further emphasizes gender differences between men and women athletes in the same sports, events, and on the same teams. That is, when the discussion of strategy focuses on how to choose the best starting order of men and women athletes to accommodate for women's slower times, or other perceived performance limitations, we are not encouraged to think about men and women as teammates and equal contributors to their team's result.

This is a version of mixed-gender events that do not challenge the "implicit message sent by sex segregation":

> imposing segregation reflects the notion that women are unable to be competitive with men and, thus, must be protected. The result is the drawing of an able/disabled binary, which only perpetuates the idea that women are lesser than men.
>
> *(Sailors, 2016: 68)*

Instead, mixed-gender competition in these events effectively maintains the "implicit message" of sex segregation – "the idea that women are lesser than men" (Sailors, 2016: 68). That mixed-gender events can reproduce and reinforce gender differences – which are often interpreted in terms of the strengths of men athletes and the limitations of women athletes – is presumably not something the IOC anticipated in its promotion of mixed-gender events as a means to achieve gender equality on the Olympic programme.

Both World Archery and the International Shooting Sport Federation (ISSF) have celebrated their mixed-gender team events (in which there are fewer requirements about the starting order of athletes by gender) as evidence of gender equality – not only in the events themselves but in their sports as a whole. According to World Archery President, Ugur Erdener,

> Mixed team competition echoes the balanced nature of the sport, reflecting the 50-50 split of men and women in the archery competition at the Olympics, and the parity in level between the world's best men and women in competition. We're also incredibly excited that archery's athletes will have the opportunity to contest a fifth gold medal in 2020.
>
> *(in Wells, 2017)*

Archery has been included on the Olympic programme at every Summer Games since Munich 1972 (after sporadic inclusion between 1900 and 1920). During that time, men and women have competed in the same number of events: individual events only from 1972 to Los Angeles 1984; and individual and team events beginning at Seoul 1988.

Making similar claims, ISSF secretary general, Franz Schreiber, explained the addition of three mixed-gender team events for Tokyo 2020:

> We want to retain 15 Olympic events, preserve equality in our three disciplines — rifle, pistol and shotgun — and offer all female and male athletes the same opportunities. Shooting is one of the oldest and most universal sports of the world; inclusion is part of our DNA.
>
> *(in PTI, 2017)*

As discussed previously, Shooting has a distinctive history at the Olympic Games (initially being a men's sport, then an open sport, and now a gender-segregated sport). Despite their historical differences, there are notable similarities in the ways that Archery and Shooting – and all of the sports included in this and the mixed-gender relay section – have added mixed-gender events to the Olympic programme: (1) these events do not require additional athletes (all mixed team event athletes must first have qualified for single-gender events); and (2) they do not require additional facilities (they use the same facilities built for the single-gender events). This explains, in part, the appeal of mixed-gender events for the IOC and the IFs; that is, the opportunity to add a medal event without needing to increase the IF's athlete quota or increase the cost of the facility. In fact, it means more use of the facility during the Games. In the case of Archery, the mixed-gender team event is also celebrated as providing an additional medal opportunity for countries that send fewer athletes to the games (like Parson's claim about the Paralympic Swimming mixed-gender relay events). Each country is able to send six athletes to the Olympic Games (three men and three women), and only countries with six athletes are able to compete in the single-gender team events (single-gender teams are made up of three athletes). The mixed-gender team event "would also allow for some smaller archery nations to field competitive pairs at an Olympics where they may not be able to qualify full teams" (Stanley, 2017). All of the IFs that have added mixed-gender relay and/or team events, with the exception of the ISSF, have benefited from this equation.

In stark contrast, the three mixed-gender team Shooting events that will debut on the Olympic programme at Tokyo 2020 will replace three men's events. According to *TPI* magazine (2017),

> After an exhaustive two-year evaluation process, the ISSF Ad-Hoc Committee recommended replacing the double trap men's event with a trap mixed gender team event, the 50m rifle prone men's event with a 10m air rifle mixed gender team event and the 50m pistol men's event with a 10m air pistol mixed gender team event.

They repeat the ISSF's claim that this proposal was developed to maintain discipline parity (the same number of events for each of the Shooting disciplines), and – most importantly for this discussion of mixed-gender events – Schreiber (ISSF secretary general) asserted: "This is a necessary change which according to the IOC needs to be done because of the gender equality in the Olympic programme" (in *TPI*, 2017). There were nine men's and six women's Shooting events at Rio 2016. The ISSF proposal, approved by the IOC, means there will be six events each for men and women and three mixed-gender events at Tokyo 2020. This sounds as if the ISSF has achieved gender equality, at least in terms of the events contested at the Olympic Games. However, no matter what definition of equality is used, removing men's events to add women's events (as discussed in Chapter 2) is not progress towards gender equality. The same is true for replacing men's events with mixed-gender events. When "gender equality" is used as the justification for the removal of men's events, this not only promotes negative feelings about gender equality (especially among men athletes competing in the events that have been removed), but it also obscures the fact that this decision is much more complex than simply, "the IOC requires this for gender equality". The complexity of balancing athlete quotas, the number of medal events, and meeting the aim of increased gender equality (among a host of other factors at play in decision-making about the Olympic programme) does not make a good "sound bite".

In the press release about the proposed changes, the ISSF recognized: "The changes necessary to achieve gender equality will probably include the loss of three beloved events that represent the past and no longer fulfil the highest standards for dynamic, growing Olympic events", and emphasized that the IOC makes the final decision about the Shooting events on the Olympic programme: "Again, we must emphasize that this decision is under the full authority of the IOC; it is not the ISSF that is making this decision" (ISSF, 2017). The ISSF, an IF whose Executive Committee and Council are approximately 83% men (-issf-sport.org) denies all responsibility for cutting men's events, and effectively downloads the responsibility for those cuts to the IOC and "gender equality". In fact, as noted, the ISSF Executive Committee made the decision based on a recommendation by the ISSF Ad-Hoc Committee after a two-year evaluation process. The ISSF Executive Committee then proposed the slate of Shooting events for Tokyo 2020 to the IOC. Unwillingness to own their decision raises doubt about the ISSF's sincerity in its attempts to achieve gender equality. All IFs prioritize maintaining their place on the Olympic programme and fight to keep (or increase) their athlete quota and number of medal events. If this struggle can be framed in terms of a positive (gender equality) rather than a negative (Shooting not meeting the IOC's current focus on youth and "urban appeal"), all the better (in spite of the event changes for Tokyo 2020, the ISSF was awarded 30 fewer quota places than at Rio 2016).

Much like the ISSF's previous decisions to limit some events to men only without adding all of the comparable events for women, the decision to replace men's events with mixed-gender team events is indisputably unfair to the athletes. Once again, athletes are made to bear the brunt of decisions in which they are not included and over which they have no control. Further, by explaining this decision as "necessary to achieve gender equality", men and women athletes are pitted against one another. Even though, in the case of Shooting and replacing men's events with mixed-gender team events, the opportunities provided by the new events benefit both men and women athletes (who have already qualified for the Games) by increasing the number of opportunities they have to compete for a medal. The ISSF is not the only IF to choose to replace existing events with mixed-gender events (e.g., World Sailing replaced both men's and women's events at Rio 2016 and Tokyo 2020 with mixed-gender events), and this raises additional questions about how mixed-gender events work to promote gender equality. Replacing men's events with mixed-gender events intensifies the mystery about both the intention and the reality of mixed-gender events as a tool to promote gender equality at the Olympic Games.

It is evident that there is much overlap in the characteristics of mixed-gender events in each of the four categories discussed in these chapters. There are also many questions about how these events promote gender equality on the Olympic programme. Before summarizing these characteristics and questions, it is important to recognize that there have been some, limited, concerns raised about the addition of mixed-gender events.

Concerns raised about mixed-gender events

Many IFs have publicly celebrated their addition of mixed-gender events in press releases and media coverage. They have used the opportunity to emphasize their commitment to gender equality, and sometimes claimed that mixed-gender events are evidence of the inherent gender equality in their sports (e.g., Archery, Shooting). For the ISSF, these claims are made in spite of gender differences and inequalities that recently existed in the Shooting events on the Olympic programme (until 2018), and their decision to eliminate men's events to add mixed-gender team events for Tokyo 2020.

One of the main concerns raised by IFs has been the expectation that they add mixed-gender events without adding any athletes to their quota. This means that mixed-gender events, with very few exceptions, are contested by athletes who have already qualified for the Olympic Games in a single-gender individual or team event and, thus, will compete in at least two events at the Games. Bob Bowman, who coached Michael Phelps and the U.S. men's team at Rio 2016, expressed this position,

> I have concerns about adding relay events and also adding individual events while keeping the roster sizes the same. The IOC has been insistent on keeping participant numbers at the same level. It doesn't make sense to add relay events in this dynamic.
>
> *(in Payne, 2017a)*

Similarly, World Athletics was cautious in its support for mixed-gender relays on the track and raised concerns about their execution:

> We should not expect the athletes entered to compete in the men's and women's 4 × 400m relays, from which the participants for the mixed relay will be naturally drawn, to compete in a third round of heats and finals for the mixed relay without allocating the appropriate space and time in the programme or enabling teams to bring additional athletes.
>
> *(in BBC Sport, 2017).*

These concerns emphasize two main points: (1) the challenge raised by trying to achieve competing *Agenda 2020* recommendations (discussed in Chapter 2); and (2) a sense on the part of the IFs that adding mixed-gender events is not really negotiable, that is, that the IOC expects the IFs to find ways to make mixed-gender events happen, regardless of the logistical issues they raise.

IFs have to figure out how to add mixed-gender events (and also women's events) without requiring additional athletes. In fact, both Athletics and Swimming – the two sports with the greatest number of athletes and events at the Summer Olympic Games – are making these decisions in the face of decreasing athlete quota numbers. World Athletics had a quota of 2,005 athletes (and no mixed-gender events) at Rio 2016, this was reduced to 1,900 athletes (with the inclusion of the 4 × 400m mixed-gender relay event) at Tokyo 2020 and further reduced to 1,810 athletes (with the addition of another mixed gender event) at Paris 2024. FINA faces similar reductions in its athlete quota, from 900 athletes (and no mixed-gender events) at Rio 2016 to 878 athletes (with the inclusion of the 4 × 100m mixed gender medley relay event) at Tokyo 2020, and down to 852 athletes at Paris 2024.

The drive, promoted by the IOC, to include mixed-gender events has superseded any concerns about what this means for athletes, such as the concerns raised by World Athletics. Ng (2014) identifies similar concerns about the Figure Skating mixed-gender team event. Specifically, Ng (2014) raises the idea of emerging strategies associated with skating or resting skaters (teams have the option to substitute skaters or couples in two disciplines for the free program), which favours countries with more athletes qualified for the Games. For example,

> Nations may prefer swapping pairs teams to allow athletes to rest. Since this is new, many countries are concerned about the impact. Especially in the case of the pairs, since their individual event begins two days after the close of the team event.
>
> *(Ng, 2014)*

The order of events, such as the mixed-gender team event taking place before the pairs event, as well as the potential to limit opportunities athletes may have to train with their single-gender team (e.g., Curling), are new issues presented by the inclusion of mixed-gender events on the Olympic programme.

The final major concern associated with the addition of mixed-gender events is about the events themselves. In some cases, this is expressed as concern about the legitimacy or authenticity of the mixed-gender events, and in other cases, the differences between the single-gender events and the mixed-gender event are highlighted. With respect to the former, Frank Busch, the U.S. national Swimming team director, "argued that instead of achieving gender equality, the mixed relay events were added 'all for entertainment purposes…. That's what it is'" (in Payne, 2017b).

The mixed-gender events in Judo and Triathlon are examples of the latter. Tokyo2020.org reported,

> the addition of the mixed team event will also have an effect on the individual competition as well as impacting team training sessions, given how different the individual and team competitions are from each other and the fact the team competition follows the individual competition. 'I think there are two completely different competitions and that will be a great challenge for the coaches too' […] Pereira [High Performance Manager, Brazilian Judo Confederation] remarked.
>
> *(What is the new judo mixed team event? 2020a).*

The suggestion that the individual and team competitions in Judo are 'completely different' refers only to their organization as single-gender individual or mixed-gender team events; there are actually no differences in how the athletes compete in the two events (e.g., same weight categories, same scoring system, same rules, etc.). In Triathlon, the mixed-gender relay event is very different from the single gender Triathlon events: "Athletes have to increase their power as the race distance is significantly shorter [300m swim, 8km cycle, and 2km run] compared to an Olympic Triathlon, which involves a 1.5km swim, a 40km cycle and a 10km run" (What is the new triathlon mixed team event?, 2020). Because of these differences, "training strategies have been modified to fit in with the many challenges the new sport presents". Iñaki Arenal, the head coach of the Spanish triathlon mixed relay team, has incorporated different training strategies at the national training camp: "Obviously for mixed relay the athletes need to be stronger and faster, so we have to change the pace of the training sessions in order to improve the power [more] than the endurance" (in What is the new triathlon mixed team event? 2020b). Because athletes are required to qualify for their single gender event in Triathlon (and also in Judo) in order to compete in the mixed gender event, athletes competing in mixed-gender events now have to train for two very different kinds of events and they have to be prepared to compete more times (and over more time) at the Olympic Games.

The Union Cycliste Internationale (UCI) is currently developing mixed gender Cycling events for potential inclusion at the Olympic Games and serves as an example of this potentially controversial process. At the Youth Olympic Games in Buenos Aries 2018, the BMX racing and freestyle park events were organized as mixed-gender team events (IOC, n.d.). Like many of the mixed-gender events discussed above, the results for both BMX events are determined by combining the results of one man and one woman (results from single-gender competitions). In 2019, the UCI added a mixed-gender team time trial event to their Road Cycling World Championships in Yorkshire, England. UCI President, David Lappartient, explained this decision:

> The Olympic movement is looking for more mixed gender events [...]. So it is likely that the one at Yorkshire will be the test event, and we are still working on the details of how the actual relay part will be done [...]. But there is a very good chance this event will eventually find its way to the Olympic Games.
>
> *(in Agence France-Presse, 2018)*

Lappartient claimed in 2018, "The mixed relay team time trial reserved for national teams is the latest step towards greater gender equality in cycling" (in Hood, 2019). The varied responses to this new mixed-gender event from the Cycling world are summarized by Best (2019): "But is it a great leap forward for equality in women's and men's racing, or—as some critics have suggested—a somewhat ill conceived publicity stunt designed to appeal to the International Olympic Committee?". Proponents of the event claim,

> It will also help bring better parity in the sport. It's combining men's and women's racing, giving them equal billing at cycling's biggest event. It'll be the women crossing the line last and it will be them afforded that first moment of sheer joy if they manage to win the inaugural title.
>
> *(Robinson, 2019)*

Opponents have questioned the selection and organization of the team time trial as a possible mixed-gender event.

In 2015, Lappartient's predecessor, Brian Cookson, seemed guarded about the potential for mixed-gender events in Cycling. Discussing the UCI's decision to test mixed-gender events, Cookson said,

> It will have to be very carefully managed. Coaches and sports scientists tell me that men are between 10 to 15 per cent faster than women in any given cycling event so we would have to find ways to moderate that difference if they are going to be competing at the same time. If it's a disaster and doesn't work, we can report back to the IOC and say we tried it but it's impractical.
>
> *Let's see (in Wynn, 2015)*

Like the ISSF, Cookson seems to emphasize pressure from the IOC as the main impetus for considering mixed-gender events. Following the decision to include the mixed-gender team time trial at the 2019 Road Cycling World Championships, Cycling insiders referred to the event as "Mickey Mouse", "contrived", and a "second category event" if the top athletes chose not to compete in order to focus on their individual events (Best, 2019). Connie Carpenter-Phinney, who won the inaugural women's road race at Los Angeles 1984, offered a damning critique of the UCI and the mixed-gender team time trial event:

> The UCI legislate how tall your socks are [but] the only time they ever legislate for the [women's] sport is when the International Olympic Committee sends down a message saying, 'we need more women in track cycling' or 'we need more parity when we get to the Olympics'. [Now the UCI appears to be] scrambling to try to create the illusion of parity, where parity doesn't exist.
>
> *(in Best, 2019)*

It is possible to extend this critique – "creating the illusion of parity, where parity doesn't exist" to all mixed-gender events organized in sports that continue to enforce different opportunities and/or conditions of participation for men and women athletes. In Cycling, some of these differences have been addressed for the events included at the Olympic Games (e.g., number of events, number of athletes on a pursuit team), while others have not (e.g., the distance of road races, the features of BMX courses). However, women cyclists in amateur and professional competitions outside the Games continue to receive drastically less pay, promotion, media coverage, and resources in general than men cyclists. If mixed-gender events are added in place of – rather than alongside – addressing the gendered differences in the already existing Cycling events, this reinforces Channon et al.'s (2016: 1114) claim, "in many contexts, the potential for transformative experiences in sex-integrated sports is thwarted or at least slowed by the persistence of deep, historically rooted and often taken-for-granted practices which marginalize women". Further, it calls into question how the addition of mixed-gender events, without explicit consideration of a sport's institutionalized gender differences, may work to promote gender equality.

Conclusion

Following the PyeongChang 2018 Winter Olympic Games, the IOC claimed that both women and gender parity had been in "the spotlight":

> Underlining the IOC's commitment to promoting parity is the fact that the Winter Games now feature a number of mixed gender events, with curling mixed doubles and the Alpine skiing mixed team event joining luge and biathlon mixed relays, and of course, the figure skating pairs, ice dance and team event on the programme at PyeongChang 2018.
>
> *(IOC, 2018)*

Notably, as discussed in Chapter 1, in their language about gender equality, the IOC has started to use "equality" and "parity" interchangeably, though parity refers only to numbers: "The goal is to reach a balanced ratio of women and men (ideally, 50/50) in terms of representation and participation at all levels. [...] it represents only a limited way to measure gender equality" (UNESCO, 2015). Even in this regard, the Luge mixed-gender relay event does not contribute to a balanced representation of men and women because it features three men and one woman. As demonstrated in this chapter, evidence indicates that the inclusion of mixed-gender events does not actually "foster gender equality", when equality is understood in terms of equal status, including opportunities, access, and benefits (UNESCO, 2015). In fact, mixed-gender events challenge – rather than promote – the goal of gender equality when they are organized in ways that reinforce gendered differences between men's and women's participation.

Among the four categories of mixed-gender events, common characteristics include (1) reproducing and reinforcing existing gender differences; (2) emphasizing gender differences in new ways that are specific to the mixed-gender events; (3) indirect mixed gender competition; and (4) no additional athletes. In many cases, mixed-gender events reproduce and reinforce the existing gender differences between men's and women's participation. This includes, but is not limited to, gender differences in race distance (e.g., Biathlon), uniforms (e.g., Figure Skating, Swimming), weight categories (e.g., Judo), and athlete weight limits (e.g., Luge). These gender differences contribute to gender inequality because, when there are differences, women always race over shorter distances, are required to wear tighter fitting and more revealing uniforms, and have lower weight allowances. This means that as IFs have devised or identified mixed-gender events to propose for inclusion on the Olympic programme, they have – universally – not taken the opportunity to address any of the gendered rules or structural differences in their sports (where these exist). The mixed-gender component of these events has largely been uncritically accepted as contributing to gender equality, without actually prioritizing the equal – in terms of status, access, opportunities, and benefits – involvement of men and women athletes in mixed-gender events.

In many mixed-gender events, gender differences are emphasized in new ways related to the organization of the event. For example, when an IF prescribes the starting order of athletes based on gender for a mixed gender event, that is, woman-woman-man-man or woman-man-woman-man (e.g., Biathlon and Triathlon). When the starting order is prescribed, it typically privileges men by ensuring that men will cross the finish line, thus winning the race for their team and receiving media and spectator attention associated with doing so. Mixed-gender events have also introduced – at the Olympic Games – a dialogue about strategy related to athletes' gender, such as strategy related to the starting order of athletes when it is not prescribed by the IF (e.g., Athletics, Swimming), or with respect to gendered roles (based on assumptions about men being stronger and women having more "finesse") on a mixed-gender team (e.g., Curling and Sailing). In these cases, the emphasis on gender differences often identifies women's abilities as a potential deficit to their team. The strategy, we are told, is about where to place the women athletes so that their lesser abilities will have the least negative effect on their team, such as in the mixed gender 4 × 400m relay in Athletics. In Wheelchair Rugby, this is extended to allowing teams an additional 0.5 classification points when they put a woman athlete on the court, which may be interpreted as an incentive to include women athletes, but also intimates that a team may be more "disabled" when a woman athlete is playing. Emphasis on gender differences, especially when those differences bolster the idea that men are naturally stronger, faster, better athletes than women, does not promote gender equality. In fact, it does exactly the opposite by reproducing and normalizing gender inequality.

Gender inequality is further reproduced through the inclusion of mixed-gender events when the mixed-gender aspect of these events is so indirect that the mixed-gender events look identical to single-gender events. When men compete against men and women compete against women in the Alpine Skiing parallel slalom mixed-gender team event and Judo mixed-gender team event, these events look exactly the same as the single-gender Alpine skiing parallel slalom and Judo events. The mixed gender component – adding together men's and women's times or scores – is not visible to spectators or viewers at home, and the relative contributions of the men and women athletes are not apparent. On a positive note, we do see men and women on the podium together, being awarded the same medal for their performances. Based on these common characteristics of mixed-gender events, it is exceedingly difficult to understand how the IOC identified mixed-gender events as a means of fostering gender equality, and why they continue to encourage IFs to add mixed-gender events to the Olympic programme. However, because the IOC has historically counted mixed-gender events only as women's events, increasing their number effectively furthers the

IOC's ability to publicize numbers that suggest the Olympic programme has achieved gender parity. This very limited and also misleading accounting of gender equality at the Olympic Games raises doubt about the IOC's sincerity in its pursuit of gender equality.

In spite of the reality, the IOC continues to promote mixed-gender events as an integral part of their gender equality accomplishments. For example, in a press release about the Paris 2024 Olympic programme, the IOC (2020b) identified the increased number of mixed-gender events: "Paris 2024 will also mark a growth in mixed events on the programme, compared to Tokyo 2020, from 18 to 22" as part of their claim that Paris 2024 will be "the first gender equal Olympic Games". Others have endorsed and/or repeated the IOC's position. Nancy Hogshead-Makar, a former American Olympic swimmer and CEO of Champion Women, argued that mixed-gender events "go a step further than simply having women's events": "When you're lifting weight for weight and swimming lap for lap, it's hard to hold the view that women are inferior. The more opportunities for men and women to be peers within sports, the better" (in Costa, 2018).

This perspective, suggesting that mixed-gender events are even more "equal" than having an equal number of women's events on the Olympic programme, advocates a potentially harmful misconception about mixed-gender events, that is, mixed-gender events are able to achieve the "promise" of sex integration detailed by Channon et al. (2016: 1112):

> In its simplest form, the fundamental 'promise' of sex integration lies in the fact that it challenges us to reject a priori assumptions of male superiority [...]. When women and men face each other as ostensible equals in athletic contests, [...] or when they rely on one another's athletic prowess for the sake of team success, the usual gendered logic stressing inevitable male predominance stands to be challenged.

The common characteristics of the mixed-gender events that have been added to the Olympic and Paralympic programmes fall short – in some cases far short – of producing conditions in which "men and women face each other as ostensible equals".

A significant barrier to fostering gender equality at the Olympic Games – whether through the addition of mixed-gender events or other means – is the current requirement that IFs find ways to add events without increasing the number of athletes at the Games. This leads to the final common characteristic of mixed-gender events on the Olympic programme: they are an additional medal event that does not require more athletes for an IF's quota. Specifically, IFs are encouraged to add mixed-gender events in which only athletes who have already qualified to compete in a single-gender event can compete. Kit McConnell, the IOC Sports Director, claims, "One of the real benefits we see in these types of events is they can fit into athlete quotas" (in Costa, 2018), which seems to suggest that the IOC places more value on achieving Recommendation 9 than

Recommendation 11 of *Agenda 2020*. Adding mixed-gender events is often in place of creating additional participation opportunities for women at the Games. This is the focus of the first strategy under Recommendation 11: "The IOC to work with the International Federations to achieve 50 percent female participation [...] by creating more participation opportunities at the Olympic Games" (IOC, 2014). Mixed-gender events may, technically, create more participation opportunities for women at the Olympic Games, but they do so only for women who already have at least one participation opportunity at the Games. In fact, at Sochi 2014, the only additional participation opportunity created was for a man singles figure skater from Great Britain (in order for Great Britain to be able to field a full team for the Figure Skating mixed-gender team event). As Costa (2018) notes, "the mixed-team events typically feature athletes that are already competing in traditional medal events. They add novelty and exposure for female athletes in the most logistically simple way possible". In what ways do "novelty and exposure" contribute to gender equality?

Mixed-gender events may contribute to increased legitimacy for women athletes at the Olympic Games, by further normalizing their participation and demonstrating their abilities alongside their men teammates. However, it is also possible that women athletes' involvement at the Games is further trivialized by the "novelty" of mixed-gender events, and their exposure as a result of these events – when it emphasizes gender differences in ways that disparage women's relative abilities – may also be trivializing. The way that mixed-gender events are currently organized results in more being expected of the women (and men) athletes who compete in them. They are asked to compete additional times (either before or after their single-gender events), on additional days, and sometimes in events that are quite different from their single-gender events (e.g., mixed gender doubles Curling, the mixed-gender team event in Triathlon). These additional demands on athletes, so that IFs and the IOC can commend themselves for improving gender equality at the Games, do not seem to support the athlete-centred focus of *Agenda 2020*. Instead, they demonstrate the ways that athletes are most affected by decisions made, often without consulting them, about the Olympic programme. This is particularly true for the athletes in single-gender events that have been removed from the Olympic programme to add mixed-gender events, such as the men athletes who compete in the double trap, 50m rifle prone, and 50m pistol Shooting events. As discussed previously, athletes did not create either "gigantism" at the Olympic Games or gender inequality on the Olympic programme; however, it is the athletes who experience the negative effects of attempts to address them.

Mixed-gender events are an improvement over open events because they require participation by both men and women athletes, and in most cases an equal number of men and women athletes. They may also influence National Olympic Committees (NOC) to invest more in their women's training programmes in sports with mixed-gender events, because in order to be successful in these events, teams must be able to field strong men and women athletes. Referring to the addition of the Biathlon and Luge mixed-gender relays and the Figure Skating team competition at Sochi 2014, Thomas (2014) claimed, "These new contests value women's contributions without focusing on gender differences in strength or speed. To win gold in a team or relay event, a nation must be blessed with outstanding male and female athletes". Though the evidence in this chapter contradicts Thomas' first claim, the second is undeniably accurate. I would suggest, however, that nations are able, to a degree, to influence whether or not they are "blessed with outstanding men and women athletes" through their investments in sport programmes for boys and girls, and men and women. IFs often claim that mixed-gender events offer a more level playing field for smaller countries than single-gender relay and team events. Thomas (2016) claims,

> Populous, rich nations with well-organized sports programs have a huge advantage in relays. It's easy enough for a vast country like the United States, population 324 million, to line up four great male or female freestylers. Mixed relays reward smaller countries that are blessed with outstanding men and exceptional women, since you only need two of each to compete.

This highlights another trend in the organization of mixed-gender events; they typically include fewer athletes than the comparable single-gender events. For example, only two athletes in mixed doubles Curling compared to four athletes in the men's and women's events, and two athletes in the Archery mixed-gender team event compared to three athletes in the men's and women's team events.

Overall, regardless of their ability to "foster gender equality", athletes seem to be generally excited about participating in mixed-gender events at the Olympic Games. Kim Boutin, who won three Short-Track Speed Skating medals for Canada at PyeongChang 2018, said about the new mixed-gender relay event that will be introduced at Beijing 2022:

> It's fun to have a new event. It will be a good show but also a good challenge. I find it interesting to mix the boys and the girls to show a country's strength as a whole, and I'm not too worried for Canada!
>
> *(in IOC, 2020a)*

Importantly, there is most often one medal available for mixed-gender events, and more than one medal available in the single-gender women's events. Nations should be investing in their women's programmes for many reasons, and potential success in mixed-gender events is not at the top of the list.

References

Agence France-Presse (29 September 2018). Mixed-gender TTT expected at Olympics after debut at worlds. https://www.velonews.com/news/mixed-gender-ttt-set-at-worlds-olympic-programme/. Retrieved: 21 February, 2021.

BBC Sport (9 June 2017). Tokyo 2020: Mixed-gender events added to Olympic Games. https://www.bbc.com/sport/olympics/40226990. Retrieved: 1 December, 2020.

Best, Isabel (23 September, 2019). Team time trial mixed relay and the debate around co-ed racing – World Championships. https://www.cyclingnews.com/features/team-time-trial-mixed-relay-and-the-debate-around-co-ed-racing-world-championships/. Retrieved: 1 December, 2020.

Channon, Anna, Katherine Dashper, Thomas Fletcher & Robert J. Lake (2016). The promises and pitfalls of sex integration in sport and physical culture. *Sport in Society*, 19(8–9), 1111–1124.

Costa, Brian (9 February 2018). Pyeongchang 2018 – Team USA: The rise of coed competitions – Why the IOC has expanded events that include both men and women in this year's Winter Games and beyond. *The Wall Street Journal*, A12.

Hood, Andrew (20 September 2019). Mixed relay world championship drawing wait-and-see attitude. https://www.velonews.com/news/road/mixed-relay-world-championship-drawing-wait-and-see-attitude/. Retrieved: 21 February, 2021.

IBU (19 December 2017). Mixed relay: It's all about the mix. https://www.biathlonworld.com/about-biathlon/disciplines/mixed-relay-it-s-all-about-the-mix. Retrieved: 13 January, 2021.

IBU maintains mixed gender drive with new World Championships discipline (2016). SportBusiness, July 8, 2016. https://www.sportbusiness.com/news/ibu-maintains-mixed-gender-drive-with-new-world-championships-discipline/. Retrieved: 24 December, 2020.

IBU (2020). *International Biathlon Union (IBU) Event and Competition Rules*. http://www.ffs.fr/pdf/reglements/REGBIATH/FFSreg-biat6a.pdf

IOC (n.d.). Olympic Programme 3rd Summer Youth Olympic Games – Buenos Aries 2018.

IOC (6 April 2011). Six new events added to the Olympic Winter Games programme in Sochi – Olympic News. https://www.olympic.org/news/six-new-events-added-to-the-olympic-winter-games-programme-in-sochi. Retrieved: 13 January, 2021.

IOC (2014). *Olympic Agenda 2020: 20 +20 Recommendations*. Lausanne: International Olympic Committee.

IOC (19 September 2018). Mixed-gender events a sign of innovation at the Youth Olympic Games. https://www.olympic.org/news/mixed-gender-events-a-sign-of-innovation-at-the-youth-olympic-games. Retrieved: 19 December, 2020.

IOC (21 November 2019). Tactics at the fore in Athletics mixed relay. https://www.olympic.org/news/tactics-at-the-fore-in-athletics-mixed-relay. Retrieved: 21 January, 2021.

IOC (28 January 2020a). Mixed events enrich the Winter Games programme. https://www.olympic.org/news/mixed-events-enrich-the-winter-games-programme. Retrieved: 21 February, 2021.

IOC (7 December 2020b). Gender equality and youth at the heart of the Paris 2024 Olympic Sports Programme. https://www.olympic.org/news/gender-equality-and-youth-at-the-heart-of-the-paris-2024-olympic-sports-programme. Retrieved: 21 February, 2021.

ISSF (20 February 2017). ISSF Press Release—ISSF Executive Committee and Administrative Council meet to discuss Tokyo 2020 Olympic Program recommendations. https://www.issf-sports.org/getfile.aspx?mod=docf&pane=1&inst=340&iist=82&file=20170220%20ISSF%20Press%20Release%2002.pdf. Retrieved: 13 January, 2021.

ITU launches Mixed Relay Series ahead of discipline's Olympic debut (11 December 2017). SportBusiness International team. https://www.sportbusiness.com/sport-news/itu-launches-mixed-relay...aily%20Newswires&pi_campaign_id=2363&utm_source=sbi-newswire-2017. Retrieved: 13 December, 2017.

Morgan, Liam (28 January 2018). Mixed gender and class relay in athletics among new Paralympic disciplines at Tokyo 2020. https://www.insidethegames.biz/articles/1060742/mixed-gender-and-class-relay-in-athletics-among-new-paralympic-disciplines-at-tokyo-2020. Retrieved: 19 December, 2020.

Ng, Callum (5 February 2014). How the Olympic figure skating team event works. https://olympic.ca/2014/02/05/how-the-olympic-figure-skating-team-event-works/. Retrieved: 6 January, 2015.

Payne, Marissa (11 April 2017a). Mixed relays? Swimming's governing body suggests adding events for 2020 Olympics. https://www.washingtonpost.com/news/early-lead/wp/2017/04/11/mixed...wimmings-governing-body-suggests-adding-events-for-2020-olympics/. Retrieved: 1 December, 2020.

Payne, Marissa (28 April 2017b). In a push for equality, IOC wants to add mixed-gender events to Olympic program. *The Washington Post*. https://www.washingtonpost.com/news/early-lead/wp/2017/04/28/in-a-p...r-equality-ioc-wants-to-add-mixed-gender-events-to-olympic-program/. Retrieved: 27 January, 2021.

Price, Karen (23 July 2019). 9 new mixed-gender events in Tokyo represent more Olympic medal opportunities for Team USA. https://www.teamusa.org/News/2019/July/23/9-New-Mixed-Gender-Eve...In-Tokyo-Represent-More-Olympic-Medal-Opportunities-For-Team-USA

PTI (24 February 2017). ISSF approves mixed gender shooting events for 2020 Tokyo Olympics. https://www.firstpost.com/sports/issf-approves-mixed-gender-shooting-events-for-2020-tokyo-olympics-3300534.html. Retrieved: 20 January, 2021.

Robinson, Joe (19 September 2019). Mixed team time trial relay: A guide to the World Championships's newest event. https://www.cyclist.co.uk/news/7098/mixed-team-time-trial-relay-a-guide-to-the-world-championshipss-newest-event. Retrieved: 21 February, 2021.

Sailors, Pam R. (2016) Off the beaten path: Should women compete against men? *Sport in Society*, 19(8–9), 1125–1137.

Stanley, John (8 June 2017). Better together: Why the mixed team is here to stay. https://worldarchery.sport/news/148967/better-together-why-mixed-team-here-stay. Retrieved: 28 January 2021.

Thomas, June (14 February 2014). Do the Olympics really need separate men's and women's curling competitions? https://slate.com/culture/2014/02/curling-2014-olympics-do-the-olympics-really-need-separate-men-s-and-women-s-curling-competitions.html.

Thomas, June (14 August 2016). Michael Phelps and Katie Ledecky in the same relay? It could happen. https://slate.com/culture/2016/08/mixed-gender-swimming-relays-are-likely-coming-to-the-olympics-hooray.html. Retrieved: 27 February, 2021.

UNESCO (June, July, August 2015). *Gender Wire – Division for Gender Equality*. No. 1.

Wells, Chris (9 June 2017). Archery's mixed team event added to Olympic programme for 2020. https://worldarchery.org/news/149072/archerys-mixed-team-event-added-olympic-programme-2020. Retrieved: January 21, 2021.

What is the new judo mixed team event? (27 November 2020a). https://tokyo2020.org/en/news/what-is-the-new-judo-mixed-team-event. Retrieved: 27 January, 2021.

What is the new triathlon mixed relay? (14 September 2020b). https://tokyo2020.org/en/news/what-is-the-new-triathlon-mixed-relay. Retrieved: 4 February, 2021.

Wynn, Nigel (17 March 2015). UCI to test mixed-gender cycling events this week. https://www.cyclingweekly.com/news/latest-news/uci-to-test-mixed-gender-cycling-events-this-week-162441. Retrieved: 21 February, 2021.

6

GRATUITOUS GENDERING, GENDER EQUALITY, AND THE OLYMPIC PROGRAMME

Foster gender equality: achieved?

In January 2021, the IOC released *Olympic Agenda 2020 – Closing Report* in which they assess the status of each of the 40 original *Agenda 2020* (IOC, 2014) recommendations as either partially achieved, mostly achieved, or achieved. The IOC (2021a) claims that 88% of the recommendations have been achieved, including Recommendation 11: "Foster gender equality". In fact, the IOC (2021a) claims it "went well beyond the set recommendation and has advanced gender equality on numerous fronts". Among those "numerous fronts" are increases to the number of women athletes participating at the Olympic Games and the number of mixed-gender events (both strategies to achieve Recommendation 11 that were included in *Agenda 2020*), and also increased representation of women in governance,[1] support for the launch of the UN Women Sports for Gender Equality Initiative, and "Other collaborations to advance Gender Equality and Inclusion" (IOC, 2021a). In Chapter 2, I discussed the increases in the number of women athletes and women's events included on the Olympic programme, and the IOC is correct to make this claim. Missing from this "achievement" is the elimination of places for men athletes and men's events that has often accompanied the increases for women athletes and women's events. As detailed in Chapters 4 and 5, it is also accurate that the number of mixed-gender events on the Olympic programme has increased since 2014; but, given the inconsistency in the organization of these events and the ways in which many mixed-gender events reinforce gender difference, it remains unclear how these events contribute to gender equality at the Games.

Finally, as addressed in Chapter 3 (and Chapters 4 and 5), Recommendation 11 did not address the significant gender inequalities that exist on the Olympic programme in the ways that men and women athletes compete in the same sports

DOI: 10.4324/9781003002741-6

and events. In some cases, these continue to be numerical, that is, when there is a difference in the number of men and women athletes in an event or men's and women's teams in a tournament, there are always fewer women athletes and teams. In many cases, and across a number of categories, these are differences in the conditions of participation for men and women athletes. These categories include differences in the length of races, available weight categories, the height, weight, size, and spacing of equipment and the size of venue, and differences in judging, rules, and uniforms. In every case where gendered differences have been institutionalized through *within* sport typing, women's participation is designed to be *less than* men's participation, such as racing over shorter distances, using lighter, shorter, smaller equipment, prohibiting elements that are allowed in the men's events, and emphasizing women's appearance by requiring more revealing uniforms. The cumulative effect of these many (sometimes small) differences cannot be ignored, and addressing these differences must be part of any strategy to achieve gender equality at the Olympic Games. In an IOC Medical Commission publication titled "Women in Sport", Pfister questioned,

> Equality in the Olympic movement: what might this signify? Interpreting equal participation with equality is problematical, not least because the sporting activities, performance and achievements of men and women have different meanings and can convey different messages. Sport, with its seemingly impartial hierarchy of achievement, contributes in no small way to the construction of the gender order, and above all to the naturalization of gender and gender differences (Théberge, 1991).
>
> *(Pfister, 2000: 17)*

While the majority of events on both the Summer and Winter Olympic sport programmes include evidence of gratuitous gendering, the IOC cannot accurately claim to have "fostered gender equality" at the Olympic Games.

Gender equality review project

In February 2018, the IOC Executive Board approved the Gender Equality Review Project (GERP), comprised of 25 "Gender Equality Recommendations". This is the closest that the IOC has come to acknowledging gender inequality at the Olympic Games *beyond* the numbers. The GERP was the result of work conducted by the IOC Women in Sport and Athletes' Commissions and 11 working group members. The working group members were all either IOC members and/or in top-level positions in International Federations (IFs) and National Olympic Committees (NOCs). Marisol Casado, president of the International Triathlon Union (ITU) served as the group's Chair. Working group members collected information through consultations with six "stakeholder groups" (athletes, NOC representatives, IF representatives, sports media professionals, academics specializing in sports studies, and business leaders from the private sector), interviews, and a review of the existing literature about gender equality and the Olympic Movement (IOC, 2018). According to IOC president Thomas Bach, "The aim of this was to provide a solutions-based approach to achieving gender equality on and off the field of play – a goal that everyone in the Olympic Movement can support" (IOC, 2018).

The 25 gender equality recommendations are divided into five categories: sport; portrayal; funding; governance; and HR, monitoring, and communications. Once again, the IOC has produced an important document about gender equality, but has not defined what it means by gender equality. In the GERP recommendations, there is evidence of an approach that goes beyond gender parity to a fuller commitment to gender equality in terms of equal status. Since the GERP recommendations were released, the IOC has made progress towards achieving some of the recommendations. For example, in the sport category, the GERP working group recommended "Equal representation of women's and men's events in the competition schedule" (IOC, 2018). Historically, there were more men's events (or only men's events) scheduled on the final day of the Olympic Games. According to the IOC (2021b),

> The middle and final weekends, and in particular the last Sunday (Day 16) of the Olympic Games, are prime global broadcasting moments. Emphasis has therefore been placed first and foremost on these prominent occasions to make the most significant improvements. In comparison to the Olympic Games Rio 2016, the last Sunday of the Olympic Games Tokyo 2020 will include a balanced number of medal events and total competition hours [for men and women].

For Beijing 2022, the "Final Saturday to feature nine hours of women's events, compared to five hours on the same day in PyeongChang four years ago" (IOC, 2022). Including gender balance as a criterion for the competition schedule is important in order to increase the visibility of women athletes and women's events during the Olympic Games. It is also consistent with the IOC's commitment to gender parity in the way that it focuses on the number of events and competition hours for men and women during "prime time" at the Games.

Importantly, the GERP working group went beyond recommending gender balance by including an entire category devoted to portrayal that considers both quantity and quality. Portrayal is defined as "The language (words and expressions), images and voices used, the quality and quantity of coverage and the prominence given, when depicting individuals or groups in communications and the media" (IOC, 2021c). The recommendations in this category are all about ensuring "fair and balanced/equal portrayal of men and women", by the IOC, by the Organizing Committees of the Olympic Games (OCOGs), and by all media (with a focus on Olympic Movement stakeholders and partners) (IOC, 2018). To this end, the IOC released *Portrayal Guidelines for Gender Balanced Representation* in 2018, and an updated *Portrayal Guidelines: Gender-equal, fair and inclusive representation in sport* in 2021. In the introduction to the second edition, the IOC (2021c) explains,

> These call for the implementation of "gender-equal and fair portrayal practices in all forms of communication" across the IOC, at the Olympic Games and throughout the Olympic Movement – whose members are, in turn, encouraged to adopt and adapt these Guidelines according to cultural contexts.

This highlights a second ongoing challenge – in addition to not offering a definition of gender equality – in the IOC's gender equality initiatives: both the GERP and the Portrayal Guidelines are framed as recommendations or guidelines (not requirements), and members of the Olympic Movement are encouraged (not obligated) to adopt them. The IOC (2021c) has provided a "Portrayal in sport checklist" that encourages "you" to "Check your content", "Check your imagery", "Check your words", and "Check your 'voices'". However, beyond statements to the effect that "The IOC believes **women's and men's events are of equal importance**, and this should be reflected in their treatment", the IOC (2021c) does not identify any consequences for organizations that do not follow the Portrayal Guidelines. The same is true of the GERP Recommendations. With only a couple of exceptions for recommendations that identify a specific timeline for achievement, the IOC Executive Board has "endorsed" the GERP Recommendations with no specific commitments about *how and by when* they will be achieved.

The answer to "How and when?" for implementation of the Gender Equality recommendations is: "The implementation phase for the recommendations has started, in close cooperation with each member of the Olympic Movement concerned. A progress review will be held at the annual meeting of the IOC Women in Sport and Athletes' Commissions". Annual progress reviews sound promising, though it is unclear how progress will be measured when there is little sense of how long it should take to achieve most of the recommendations or the criteria used to assess progress. In the *Olympic Agenda 2020 – Closing Report*, the IOC (2021a) claims,

> A review of the implementation of the 25 recommendations in January 2020 highlighted that extensive progress have been made (e.g. balancing competition schedule to give equal prominence to female and male athletes and publication of IOC Portrayal Guidelines for the benefit of entire Olympic Movement) but that substantial work remains to close the gender gap (e.g. female representation in coaches and technical officials accredited to the Olympic Games as well as on governing bodies in the Olympic Movement).

There have been no updates about what progress has been made with respect to the recommendations that are most relevant to studying gender equality and the

Olympic programme. Included in the sport category, these recommendations address many of the gender inequalities – quantitative and qualitative – that are detailed in the previous chapters. Of note, despite their prominence in Recommendation 11 and the IOC's reporting about gender equality achievements, there is no mention of mixed-gender events in the GERP Recommendations.

The first sport-focused recommendation is aligned with, but goes further than Recommendation 11:

1 Recommendation: **Olympic Games Participation**
   - Ensure there is full gender equality in athlete quotas and medal events for both genders from the Olympic Games 2024 and the Olympic Winter Games 2026 onwards.
   - For all team sports/disciplines/events, ensure an equal number of teams and, where appropriate, an equal number of athletes for both genders.
   - For all individual events, the number of female and male participants should be equal per event and/or per discipline (IOC, 2018).

   This is the first time that the IOC has made reference to gender equality in numbers *beyond* the total number of athletes and the total number of events at the Olympic Games. It is curious that the GERP working group identified a specific date by which IFs and the IOC should ensure gender equality in athlete quota and event numbers, but there are no recommended dates for the review of the numbers of teams, numbers of athletes on teams, and athletes in events. This is likely related to the IOC's position (enshrined in the *Olympic Charter*) that as long as they comply with specific IOC requirements, "each IF maintains its independence and autonomy in the governance of its sport".

   Additional recommendations focus specifically on the conditions of participation in sports and events in which both men and women compete. In Chapter 3, I detailed examples of the existing differences that lead to these recommendations:

2 Recommendation: **Competition Formats and Technical Rules**
   - Ensure the competition formats related to distances, duration of competition segments, number of rounds, etc. between women and men are as equal as possible.

3 Recommendation: **Uniforms**
   - Ensure that competition uniforms reflect the technical requirements of the sport and do not have any unjustifiable differences.

4 Recommendation: **Equipment/Apparatus**
   - As much as possible, the sport-specific equipment and apparatus for men and women should be the same.

     [...]

7 Recommendation: **Venues and Facilities**
   - That women and men use the same venues and fields of play where possible.

The GERP Recommendations document does not include references to any of the reviewed literature, and it is important to point out that Donnelly and Donnelly (2013) and Donnelly et al. (2015) made many of these same recommendations in gender audit reports about the London 2012 and Sochi 2014 Olympic Games. Also salient is the qualifying language used in these recommendations, such as "where possible", "as much as possible", "as equal as possible", and "unjustifiable differences", which implies that there are justifiable differences in men's and women's uniform requirements. This appears to be ongoing evidence of the IOC's *accommodating women* approach to gender equality. Specifically, the Gender Equality Recommendations simultaneously call into question examples of *within* sport typing on the Olympic programme and leave room to affirm the IOC and IFs' "binary and hierarchical notions of gender difference" (Pape, 2020: 82).

Within sport typing at the Olympic Games bolsters, as Pfister (2000) claimed, "the naturalization of gender and gender differences". Gender Equality Recommendations 2, 3, 4, and 7 are intended to address the gratuitous gendering of sports and events on the Olympic programme. Pape (2020: 100) argues that the sex-segregated organization of sport at the Olympic Games "established women's lesser status and ability as an organizational norm". This ensures that men and women do not compete directly against each other, and even the increasing number of mixed-gender events on the Olympic programme have, for the most part, continued to support this strategy. The variety and extent of the differences constructed into the ways that men and women athletes compete in the same sports and events are gratuitous when the women's version of participation is designed to reinforce stereotypical notions of femininity (and, by extension, masculinity). A second major purpose of this gratuitous gendering seems to be to guarantee that men's and women's performances cannot be compared, which leaves the perceived superiority of men athletes and men's events largely unchallenged. The necessity and/or "justifiability" of *within* sport typing is challenged because it is not consistent across sports and events on the Olympic programme. When men and women triathletes and marathon runners compete over the same distances, their participation calls into question the unequal race distances contested by men and women biathletes and road cyclists, among others. Further, when the ISSF is able to eliminate the gratuitous gendering of equipment (pistols, rifles, and shotguns) and structure of Shooting events (number of shots and length of time) with no apparent consequences for athletes' performances, the legitimacy of those enforced differences becomes even more suspect. At the same time, Shooting provides a cautionary example – in the ISSF's decision to eliminate three men's events to add three mixed-gender events to the Tokyo 2020 Olympic programme – of asking IFs to take action to achieve IOC-determined recommendations without relevant guidance to ensure an athletes-first approach.

Without an IOC-provided definition of gender equality, and no guidance from the IOC (and the GERP working group), IFs are left to determine *how* to achieve the Gender Equality Recommendations, as well as how to prioritize these recommendations relative to the not-yet achieved *Agenda 2020* recommendations, and the 15 recommendations of the IOC's *Olympic Agenda 2020+5* (released in early 2021). The case of Recommendation 11 demonstrates that leaving these decisions entirely to the IFs has proven to be not only ineffective but also problematic. In particular, the IOC has created the situation that has resulted in IFs making the decision to eliminate places for men athletes and men's events to add places for women athletes and women's events in the name of gender equality and achieving the goals of *Agenda 2020*. The IOC has not only created this situation, but it has also promoted these decisions and claimed them as gender equality achievements. This ignores the fact that any meaningful commitment to gender equality has to include both men and women, and not be at the expense of men. Further, the IOC needs to determine and publicize its own priorities. It is apparent throughout this analysis of the Olympic programme that rather than being equally important, some *Agenda 2020* recommendations have been given precedence over others. While the IOC has strictly enforced Recommendation 9, by limiting the number of athletes at Paris 2024 to 10,500, Recommendation 11 has not been enforced. It is within these IOC-imposed constraints that IFs have had to figure out how to both add and reduce their athlete and event numbers. Finally, current and former athletes must be included in any decisions that are made about changing sports and events on the Olympic programme. Athletes are most directly affected by these changes and bear no responsibility for the so-called "problems" the changes are intended to solve.

Analysing the Olympic programme in detail reinforces McLachlan's (2016: 479) claim that "the Olympic movement has potentially both empowered and oppressed women, and the Olympic Games can be read or interpreted as both a site of social progress and of social constraint". There is no question that the Olympic Games are closer to achieving gender equality than ever before; however, it has taken 120 years to arrive at this point. And, it is imperative that the IOC is not allowed to claim to have achieved gender equality – as it did in the case of women comprising 48.8% of all athletes at Tokyo 2020 – when it clearly has not. While it is valuable to assess the IOC on its own terms, gender parity (or, in the IOC's words, gender balance) is only one part of gender equality. Celebrating women's inclusion at the Games, both in sports or events for the first time and in greater numbers in existing sports and events on the Olympic programme, is understandable. It becomes harmful when those inclusion narratives are the end, rather than the beginning, of the story about making progress towards gender equality. It is necessary to investigate the ways in which women have been included (or accommodated), as well as what their inclusion means for men at the Olympic Games.

Note

1 With respect to gender equality achievements in governance, the IOC (2021a) highlights that "Women represent 38% of IOC Members in 2020 [...]. Women also represent 37% of IOC Commission Chairs and 48% of IOC Commission Members". Based on the IOC membership list that was publicly available at the time of this

announcement (May 2020), I calculated that this meant that 39 women IOC members made up 47.7% of IOC commission membership (122 committee positions), and 65 men IOC members made up 52.3% of IOC commission membership (132 committee positions). If those positions were divided equally among IOC members (which is not the case), men IOC members served on about two committees each (2.03), and women IOC members served on three committees each (3.13). In order to have "female voice" heard (Bach's term), women IOC members are being asked to do more than their men counterparts; and the exclusive focus on numbers obscures this labour inequality.

References

Donnelly, Peter & Michele K. Donnelly (2013). *The London 2012 Olympics: A Gender Equality Audit*. Centre for Policy Studies Research Report. Toronto: Centre for Sport Policy Studies, Faculty of Kinesiology and Physical Education, University of Toronto.

Donnelly, Michele K., Mark Norman & Peter Donnelly (2015). *The Sochi 2014 Olympics: A Gender Equality Audit*. Centre for Policy Studies Research Report. Toronto: Centre for Sport Policy Studies, Faculty of Kinesiology and Physical Education, University of Toronto.

IOC (2014). *Olympic Agenda 2020: 20 +20 Recommendations*. International Olympic Committee: Lausanne.

IOC (2018). IOC gender equality review project: IOC gender equality recommendations – Overview. https://library.olympics.com/Default/doc/SYRACUSE/173435/ioc-gender-equality-review-project-ioc-gender-equality-recommendations-overview-international-olympi?_lg=en-GB

IOC (2021a). Olympic Agenda 2020 – Closing Report. https://stillmed.olympics.com/media/Document%20Library/OlympicOrg/IOC/What-We-Do/Olympic-agenda/Olympic-Agenda-2020-Closing-report.pdf?_ga=2.262983044.928947499.1654486323-2109730613.1619993075.

IOC (25 July 2021b). Tokyo 2020: A New blueprint for the Olympic competition schedule and the visibility of women's sport. https://olympics.com/ioc/news/tokyo-2020-a-new-blueprint-for-the-olympic-competition-schedule-and-the-visibility-of-women-s-sport. Retrieved: 29 July, 2021.

IOC (2021c). Portrayal Guidelines: Gender-equal, fair and inclusive representation in sport. https://library.olympic.org/Default/Portal/recherche/openfind.svc/GetOpenfindSelectionPdf/SELECTION_67ad76e0-2170-42be-b0c4-ded3ab500d06

IOC (14 February 2022). Beijing 2022 sets new records for gender equality. https://olympics.com/ioc/news/beijing-2022-sets-new-records-for-gender-equality. Retrieved: 1 March, 2022.

McLachlan, Fiona (2016). Gender politics, the Olympic Games, and Road Cycling: The case for critical history. *The International Journal of the History of Sport*, 33(4), 469–483.

Pape, Madeleine (2020). Gender segregation and trajectories of organizational change: The underrepresentation of women in sport leadership. *Gender & Society*, 34(1), 81–105.

Pfister, Gertrud (2000). Women and the Olympic games. In Barbara L. Drinkwater (Ed.), *Women in Sport: Volume VIII of the Encyclopaedia of Sports Medicine* (pp. 3–19). Oxford: Blackwell Science Ltd.

INDEX

Note: **Bold** page numbers refer to tables and page numbers followed by "n" denote endnotes.